Acknowledgments

Many thanks to Fred Bay and the Josephine Bay Paul and C. Michael Paul Foundation for their generous financial support of this project.

I want to express my admiration for and gratitude to all of the dedicated teacher-researchers who participated in this work.

Thanks to my dean at Seattle University, Dr. Sue Schmitt, for her support of my efforts in this project.

Many thanks to Tom Koerner at Scarecrow both for his interest in publishing this volume and for his support of my work over many years, and to Kate Kelly at Scarecrow both for her interest in the book and her gracious professionalism.

Improving Teaching in the High School Block Period

David Marshak

The Scarecrow Press, Inc.
A Scarecrow Education Book
Lanham, Maryland, and London
2001

SCARECROW PRESS, INC.

Published in the United States of America
by Scarecrow Press, Inc.
4720 Boston Way, Lanham, Maryland 20706
http://www.scaroweducation.com

4 Pleydell Gardens, Folkestone
Kent CT20 2DN, England

British Library Cataloguing in Publication Information Available

Library of Congress Cataloging-in-Publication Data
Marshak, David
    Improving teaching in the high school block period / David Marshak and Amy Chertok . . .
[et al.].   p. cm.
    Includes bibliographical references.
    ISBN 0-8108-3923-7 (paper : alk. paper)
    1. Block scheduling (Education)—United States—Case studies. 2. High school teaching—United
States—Case studies. I. Title.
    LB3032.2 .M38 2001
    373.12'42'0973—dc221

                                                                00-064090

Contents

Introduction

During the past decade thousands of American high schools have adopted block period schedules, with periods of 75, 90, or 100 minutes, or even longer. And tens of thousands of high school teachers began the task of learning how to teach effectively in a longer block of time.

What many skilled, dedicated, and creative teachers have discovered is that the block period both invites and requires good teachers to continue to develop and improve their teaching skills. One could argue that this is true of short periods, too—and to some extent it is—but the expanse of the block period, the challenge to keep students engaged over an hour and a half, the fewer class meetings in the semester or year, and the rich potential for creativity and innovation provided by the longer period all combine to offer a more profound challenge—and opportunity—to high school teachers.

This book describes how 11 high school teachers in public high schools in the Seattle area chose to take advantage of this opportunity and respond to this challenge, through self-directed professional development. Each of these teachers, some working alone and some collaborating with colleagues, chose to use the tools of action research to learn more about the effectiveness of their own teaching in block periods and to improve their own teaching and, in some cases, the teaching of their colleagues, as well.

The first two action research studies in this volume focus on the transition that students make from a middle school, with short periods, to a four-year high school with 100-minute block periods:

- Janae Hodge, a Spanish teacher, and Amy Chertock, Sarah McFarlane, and Merilee Norton, all social studies teachers, wanted to learn more about how teachers could help ninth graders who were new to block periods adapt successfully to these longer classes, which were twice the length of their middle school periods. Their findings describe a set of practices that both students and teachers perceived to be valuable for ninth graders in a block period high school.

- High school science teacher Toni Roberts chose to study how a series of related innovations in curriculum, classroom practices and organizational structures, and teaching/learning activities affects the learning and achievement of the ninth grade students in her Integrated Physical Science classes, which consisted of 100-minute block periods. Her results identify specific ways to promote ninth graders' engagement, responsibility, and learning.

The next action research studies explore a variety of issues focusing on instructional planning for the block period and innovative and complex uses of time within the longer period:

- Allen Olson, a high school science teacher, examined the variety and sequencing of teaching/learning activities in his block period classes. He articulates a set of practical insights about how to create efficient, effective sequences of varied teaching/learning activities in the block period.

- High school social studies teacher David Sherman explored his students' use of the Internet as a research vehicle as they prepared for their participation in a United Nations conference simulation. He also investigated how to use performance rubrics to encourage all students to become more active and vocal in their participation in this simulation, encourage his students to explore and apply problem-solving skills, and nurture effective collaboration among his students before and during the simulation. He offers specific understandings and insights in relation to each element in his complex study.

- Tracy Stoops, a high school biology teacher, investigated the ways in which the 100-minute block period facilitated the integration of *work world components* into high school science classes. These components included job shadowing, bringing scientists into the high school classroom to assist with complex labs and make presentations, and engaging students in conducting labs that simulate work world research. Her findings describe how each of these *work world components* can be integrated effectively into block period science classes and what their value is to students and teachers.

- Amy Chertock, a social studies teacher, and Jennifer Evans, an English teacher, both teach in the alternative education program at Shorewood High School, which serves students who are at risk. They sought to discover how they could better use the 100-minute block period to increase their students' motivation to participate constructively and learn. Their study details five strategies that promote greater student engagement and success in high school for this population of students.

- In a second study, Tracy Stoops, investigated her mostly twelfth-grade marine biology students' experience teaching lessons about whales to children in the primary grades, with an emphasis on both her students' academic learning as they prepared to teach and on her students' valuing of this cross-age tutoring opportunity. Her results illustrate how to structure this kind of cross-age tutoring within a block period structure and how this activity can encourage high school students' learning.

The next action research study explores structural innovations in a high school program coupled with 100-minute block periods:

- High school English teacher Marianne Winter Lang teaches in a two-year *looping* Integrated Program in which English, science, and social studies are interconnected, and in a traditional high school structure with separate, unrelated courses. She and her team colleagues teach the same students for ninth and tenth grades. She wanted to explore the effects of this structure on students' perceptions of their learning, their attitudes, and their motivation. Her findings compare data from students in the Integrated Program with data from students in her regular classes and identify several significant positive outcomes that result from the Integrated Program's structural innovations.

The final action research study describes an innovative model for improving teaching and learning in secondary school block periods through the activities of an *instructional coach*:

- Liz Mathewson, a veteran high school English teacher who became a *secondary school instructional coach*, explored how and to what extent she could help her teaching colleagues to use active learning strategies effectively in their block period classes. She describes in detail the many ways that a colleague acting as an *instructional coach* can help secondary teachers to improve and enrich their teaching practices.

PART 1

Ninth Graders and the Block Period

1

Transitions: Helping Ninth Graders Adapt Successfully to Block Periods

Amy Chertock, Janae Hodge, Sarah McFarlane, and Merilee Norton
Shorewood High School

Janae Hodge, a Spanish teacher, and Sarah McFarlane, Amy Chertock, and Merilee Norton, all social studies teachers, wanted to learn more about how teachers could help ninth graders who were new to block periods adapt successfully to these class durations that were twice the length of their middle school periods. They gathered data from eighth and ninth grade students and from teachers of eighth and ninth graders. Their findings describe a set of practices that both students and teachers find valuable for ninth graders in a block period high school, including posting and reviewing daily, weekly, and even monthly plans for the class; teaching time management and organizational skills; providing purposeful, well-structured breaks; incorporating a variety of teaching/learning activities into each block period; and several others.

Rationale for the Study

We are a group of teachers who have engaged in earlier research, both formal and informal, into use of the 100-minute block period. Some of us teach primarily ninth graders, and we have witnessed many struggles and challenges unique to these students, some of which are related to 100-minute periods. The most significant concern about our ninth graders that we identified, and are working on at the school and district levels, is their high rate of failure, especially in the first semester. Specific problems that relate to this failure rate and to too many ninth graders performing below their potential include the following:

- students not being able to pay attention for the whole period
- students' lack of time management skills
- students' difficulty in seeing the long-term impact of their current choices

- students not meeting deadlines for homework assignments and losing more credit because each assignment in an ABC block period schedule is for two days work
- students lacking the skills to break large assignments into manageable steps; this lack can be disastrous in an ABC block schedule because classes meet only three times a week, and teachers regularly give fewer but larger assignments

We worked out a rudimentary plan last spring to cooperate on an action research study. Our intent was to explore the impact of the 100-minute period on ninth graders, and, in particular, what teachers can do to ease the transition for students to the 100-minute schedule and to Shorewood High School in general. Rather than focus entirely on the problems, we wanted this research to be an opportunity to identify and develop solutions, which led to our guiding question:

> What can teachers do to help Shorewood ninth graders adapt success-fully to the 100-minute class period?

School Setting

Shorewood is a comprehensive high school with 1,625 students in grades 9–12. It is one of two high schools in the Shoreline School District, a suburban community of about 50,000 located directly north of Seattle, Washington. Students at Shorewood come from a wide range of socioeconomic and cultural backgrounds. About 29 percent of the students are persons of color. Almost 90 percent of students continue their education after graduation, with about half attending a four-year institution. Shorewood High School just completed its fifth year operating on an ABC block schedule: four days with three 100-minute periods ("A" days are Monday and Wednesday, "B" days are Tuesday and Thursday) and one day of traditional 50-minute periods ("C" days are on Friday). When the school week is shortened (holidays, snow days), the "C" is dropped. We also have a 25-minute period each A and B day during which students can see teachers on an individual basis.

Research Methodology

We have labeled each phase of the study with a letter. This allows the reader to follow a given phase of the study through the methodology and findings sections and in the appendixes.

A. Survey of Shorewood Ninth Graders—Last Spring

To begin to gather background information and to get ninth graders' input on how they're adjusting to the 100-minute periods we developed and administered a ninth grade student survey (appendix A). Our goals for this survey were to gather information about current ninth graders' perspectives on the block period, and to develop our own research skills so that we would have better instruments for the eighth grade survey, the focus groups, and the future ninth grade survey. All ninth graders completed the survey in early May at a special assembly during the week of state testing.

B. Focus Group with Eighth Grade Teachers—Last Spring

We randomly selected a set of eighth grade teachers from our feeder school, Einstein Middle School, and asked them to participate in a focus group. The purpose of this focus group was to elicit the teachers' observations about their students' current qualities as learners and to gather their input about what both eighth and ninth grade teachers could do to prepare students for the change in schedule that occurs at the high school (appendix B). This focus group took place at Einstein Middle School in mid-May, with four Einstein teachers participating.

C. Focus Group with Ninth Grade Teachers—Last Spring

We also decided to talk with current ninth grade teachers and randomly selected several people to participate in a focus group. The purpose of this focus group was to gather more input about what these teachers identified as problems with 100-minute periods that ninth graders experience and what they would like to see eighth grade teachers do to help ease the transition into block scheduling. We were also interested in what the Shorewood teachers thought was working and what they would like to see change for the ninth graders under the current schedule (appendix C). This focus group took place at Shorewood High School in early June, with five Shorewood teachers participating.

D. Focus Group with Ninth Grade Students—Last Spring

To learn from last year's ninth graders, we conducted a pizza party focus group with 13 students who represented a cross-section of the Shorewood ninth grade population. Our goals were to gather information about students' experiences with the 100-minute period and to encourage reflection on what both students and teachers could do to make the transition more successful (appendix D). The 13 students were divided into two focus groups, which were conducted at Shorewood High School in mid-June.

E. Survey of Einstein Eighth Graders—Last Spring

After hearing from ninth grade students and teachers and eighth grade teachers, we recognized a need to hear the eighth grade student perspective on schedules. We devised a survey and introduced it by asking students to reflect on the varying schedules they had experienced throughout their schooling. Approximately 150 eighth graders completed the survey in May, and we selected 34 surveys randomly for analysis. It should be noted that at the time we conducted the survey, students had experienced 100-minute periods recently because of a two-week window for state-mandated testing.

The goal of this particular survey was to gain an understanding of students' preferred modes of learning, including type, number, and length of activities. We also encouraged the eighth grade students to predict what the 100-minute periods would be like for them and to consider what they could do to prepare themselves for the transition to the high school's 100-minute block period schedule. Appendix E contains a copy of this survey.

F. Survey of Shorewood Ninth Graders—This Fall

Very early in this school year, we were eager to learn the initial reactions of the new ninth graders to the 100-minute block period schedule. We drew up a brief survey, which can be found in appendix F. The survey was conducted in October in three different subject areas: English, health, and world geography. These three courses are required and heterogeneous, so they constitute a random sample of the ninth grade class.

Findings

A. Survey of Shorewood Ninth Graders—Last Spring

In the initial stages of our data collection phase we decided it would be valuable to survey the current ninth graders. We wanted to test-run a survey to determine the usefulness of its questions and elicit pertinent and helpful information from the students. In addition, we wanted to receive some initial (and, as it turned out, voluminous) input on their perspectives on 100-minute periods.

Immediately after administering the survey we had some concerns. The ineffectiveness of the venue for the survey was instantly apparent to us; many students talked or grumbled, and the proctors witnessed surveys being passed back and forth between students as they completed them. As the four of us looked at the data, it became apparent that many of the students had not taken the survey seriously.

The schedule for two weeks of state-mandated testing had allowed students to sleep in. However, on the day we conducted the survey, students were forced to come in at the regular school start time for an all-ninth grade meeting, a state-mandated survey on drugs and alcohol, and then our survey. Students were resentful for having to come in early, as they perceived it. The site of the morning's events was the auditorium, where all 420 ninth graders were assembled. The students exhibited a disaffected air and did not seem to feel they had a stake in providing helpful feedback. When we read the survey results, we felt that many students, though not all by any means, either didn't believe or didn't care that their opinions would be considered.

Bearing this bias in mind, we still felt that we were able to glean some useful data and lessons from this survey. In analyzing the data, we developed three informative uses for these results:

- Pitfalls to avoid when carrying out a survey
- A comparison of the two surveys taken by two different sets of ninth graders (last spring and this fall)
- Findings from the responses of students who completed the survey in good faith

Pitfalls to avoid when carrying out a survey

First of all, we learned to keep questions very focused. Several of our questions were far too open-ended, so it was difficult to recognize trends and patterns in students' responses. We also learned to write questions that offered students an opportunity to respond to an open-ended query with their own measurable or quantifiable, yet original, responses. For example, in our initial ninth grade survey, we asked students to pick two of their classes, one that they thought used the 100 minutes effectively and one that did not. We asked them to tell us about the structure of these classes, broken down by the Beginning, Middle, and End of the class. The responses were so varied and vague that we were not able to glean any useful data or patterns from them. In contrast, however, were two questions we asked: "What is the best thing about 100-minute periods?" and "What is the worst thing about 100-minute periods?" Despite the limited nature of this question, it was much more useful because it elicited concise and measurable student-generated responses.

What we learned from the venue of the survey was that students must be in a setting with which they are familiar and where they feel comfortable. The survey would best be conducted by a teacher they know and in whom they feel a sense of trust and accountability. We also realized that it should be administered during a part of the day that is considered routine by students, so it wouldn't feel like an extra burden to them.

A comparison of the two surveys taken by two different sets of ninth graders (last spring and this fall)

What jumped out at us was that in comparing last year's and this year's ninth graders, the students' most basic reactions to the 100-minute periods were very different (with 83 respondents from each group).

Ninth Graders—Last Spring	*Ninth Graders—This Fall*
Love them (block periods): 3	Love them: 12
Like them: 27	Like them: 63
Neutral: 36	Neutral: 23
50 minutes is better: 14	Don't like them: 2
Hate them: 16	Hate them: 0

We are inclined to attribute the more negative response last spring largely to the venue and conditions in which the survey was conducted. However, we want to note that the data for each of these surveys were collected at different times of the year in different school years. Perhaps some ninth grade teachers changed their instructional practices this year to increase student engagement and interest. Perhaps some teachers became more skilled at making students more comfortable in the 100-minute periods. Or perhaps teachers are better at using class time effectively in the beginning of the school year while we are still fresh from summer break. Our results don't allow us to determine which of these applies.

Next, we compared student responses to the question, "What is the best and worst thing about the 100-minute periods?" Four trends we noticed on the positive side were that students felt "it gives us more time for homework," "there is more time to get work done," "you only have half of your classes each day," and "we learn more/learn better/can expand our learning." We were delighted that these positive observations made by students focused primarily on how the 100-minute period improves the quantity and quality of their learning. Even though student attitudes toward the 100-minute period were quite different across the two surveys, the majority of students from each group were very much in line with each other in their assertion that the best argument for 100-minute periods was their effect on their learning.

There was also similarity in the responses students gave in both surveys concerning the worst things about the 100-minute periods. The four most common responses were that the periods were "too long," "boring," "monotonous if there is no break," and "the teacher talks too long." Overall, there were fewer clusters of high numbers of responses for any particular "worst thing," especially when compared to students' responses to the "best thing." In other words, more students were able to come up with original positive comments about 100-minute periods than negative ones.

Finally, in both surveys we compared the advice that students wanted to offer teachers. The most frequent advice in both surveys was to "give breaks." We certainly heard this call in every forum for student voice our data collection allowed! (For ideas on how to incorporate breaks into the block period in a meaningful and purposeful way that increases student learning, see the Action Plan toward the end of our study.) Another strong request that emerged from the students' responses was to vary the learning activities within the class period. Students said this with a variety of suggestions: "keep us busy and engaged"; "don't do just one thing all period"; "more movement/hands-on activities"; "create variety"; "more physical activity"; and "more interactive lessons."

Findings from the responses of students who completed the survey with good faith

One insight we gained from the data that students supplied us on this survey had to do with these ninth graders' perceptions about the use of 100-minute periods in relation to classroom activities. Students were given a list of 10 general types of activities that commonly occur in class and were asked to circle those they felt took place in typical 100-minute periods. Students were not limited in the number of activities they could circle. We found that with 83 students responding:

- 63 chose Note taking
- 54 chose Group Work
- 53 chose Teacher Lecture
- 43 chose All Group Discussion
- 42 chose Individual Reading or Writing
- 35 chose Viewing Videos
- 23 chose Hands-on Activities
- 21 chose Research
- 19 chose Student Presentations
- 11 chose Learning Games

That the numbers for such teacher-centered activities as Note taking and Teacher Lecture were so high, and student-centered activities such as Student Presentations and Learning Games so low, was a bit surprising to us, given our own perceptions of the kinds of teaching/learning activities that we and our colleagues use in ninth grade classrooms. While it could be that the ninth grade teachers use more teacher-centered methods than we had thought, we realized that there might be a disconnect between students' and teachers' perceptions of the types of learning activities that take place in the classroom. For example, a teacher might ask students to read a primary source document with a partner, discuss reactions to the reading in a group of four taking notes about the discussion, and come to the board and write one comment from the group; then she/he might follow these activities with a whole class discussion. The teacher could perceive this instructional sequence as a varied group of student- and teacher-centered activities, while students might focus on this set as a teacher-led discussion with note taking. With this awareness in mind, we intend to communicate more directly with our students about the variety and purpose of activities we use in our classrooms.

B. Focus Group with Eighth Grade Teachers—Last Spring

Since our goal is to help students make a successful transition from 50-minute periods to 100-minute periods, we wanted to speak with those people who worked most closely with the young people we'd be teaching the following year as ninth graders. The information we gathered from these eighth grade teachers fell into two categories: concerns and advice. The concerns expressed had to do with developmental stages, time management skills, and at-risk students. The advice focused on the use of varied instructional strategies and ideas for teaching students how to succeed in block periods.

Many comments concerning a successful transition from 50- to 100-minute class periods focused on what could be called the *squirrel factor*, the developmental stage of many eighth graders. Many early adolescents have a short attention span and a strong need to move about. One teacher commented, "The middle school body is a different kind of animal; if a student doesn't move every seven seconds, it's amazing." The teachers agreed that because of this short attention span and constant need for movement, 100-minute periods could be a disadvantage. In contrast, the removal of the "choppy" six-period day and the reduction of "settling in and packing up" time were viewed positively by these teachers. In light of these insights we believe that ninth grade teachers should use multiple and varied teaching/learning activities in each 100-minute period and develop transition skills to move students smoothly from one activity to another with a minimum of disruption. These practices can help teachers to work effectively with ninth graders' short attention spans and their need for movement.

Another concern was students' time management skills. These teachers all believed that students needed to be taught the skills of time management explicitly. They felt that our homework policies needed to be crafted to take into account the fact that new ninth graders are unfamiliar with an ABC block schedule, with each class not meeting every day. Strategies suggested included giving new ninth graders time to adjust; not having so much homework for the first couple of weeks; explicitly teaching time management skills; and realizing that ninth graders need to be treated differently from older students. Ninth graders needed to be taught to realize that 100-minute periods count for two days of work. One way this can be achieved is if we, as ninth grade teachers, agree to teach our new students how to use the *Time-Trackers* assignment calendars they receive at the beginning of the year.

The group of teachers we interviewed from our feeder school believed that ninth grade teachers need to give students of concern—those without any time management skills, with low motivation, with little support at home—even more explicit instruction. Because the high school setting allows for more freedom and demands more responsibility than the middle school, these students need to be treated differently from older students to help them achieve success.

Finally, when asked the question, "What advice would you give the ninth grade teachers about how to ease the transition for these incoming ninth graders, particularly with respect to 100-minute periods," we received several interesting comments. The middle school teachers explained that we needed to "visually show students that it's [100 minutes] two periods" and to "purposefully teach about the use of time and scheduling." They agreed that ninth graders "need more hand holding rather than the 'sink or swim' philosophy." They also believed that ninth grade teachers need professional development in instructional pacing and transition techniques and in knowledge of the developmental stage of most early ninth grade students. This last notion was seen as extremely important because, as one teacher put it, "They're more like eighth graders than tenth graders, especially at the beginning of the year." Another commented, "You need a core group of teachers teaching ninth grade who recognize that issue."

C. Focus Group with Ninth Grade Teachers—Last Spring

In our teacher focus group at Shorewood, teachers raised five principal issues. The first one was a major difference between eighth and ninth grades in terms of homework expectations, especially deadlines. One teacher lamented, "I wasn't very successful this year. In the first two months of school I was very strict on late work, and 75 percent of my kids were failing." Ninth graders would benefit from understanding the culture and expectations of high school earlier, because now they're struggling with this new set of rules.

Directly related to this first concern were time management issues. Speaking about the best approach for helping ninth graders with time management, one teacher stated, "We must assume they don't have the ability." Another interjected that he finds "100-minute periods exacerbate issues of lack of organization. It's harder for kids to break it up, you really have to overtly teach it [time management skills]." Even the most advanced students can benefit from work on these skills. According to one teacher, the schedule hurts less motivated, lower-skilled students. It's harder for them to organize themselves, because of the day in between most class meetings. "I assign work on Monday; they do it Wednesday during lunch, so they skip a day from when they learned it [the skill/concept]." The same teacher acknowledged that there are benefits for students with high motivation: "Extra time with the teacher in class is a benefit for them, for the motivated kids."

The next issue we found in the data dealt with instructional practices and allocation of time within each 100-minute period. The length of time devoted to each activity is a variable that teachers can control and, thus, help students better adjust to 100-minute periods. One teacher recommended tailoring activities to help students develop longer attention spans. An example might be holding a class discussion for 15 minutes at the start of the year and, by second semester, extending the discussion to 25–30 minutes.

Relationships and rapport with students was another issue highlighted by the Shorewood teacher focus group. Several focus group members felt that teachers building relationships with students was one of the most helpful supports for a ninth grader. Students come from eighth grade to a huge high school and often feel lost. Whether the schedule is one of 50-minute periods or 100-minute periods, teachers need to make an extra effort at "being there for students," and making an "interpersonal connection" with them. Some teachers were frustrated with the 100-minute schedule because they did not get to see their students every day; other teachers found the long periods to be beneficial because the longer time span allowed for more individual relationships to develop between students and teacher. One teacher spoke of his in-class *Big Brother/Big Sister Program* in which seniors mentored ninth graders. He has two seniors in each of his ninth grade classes as aides. This teacher's program will be piloted next school year at Shorewood in several other ninth grade classrooms.

Several teachers also noted that it is essential for ninth grade teachers to engage students in a variety of classroom activities, particularly with the 100-minute block period. Teachers suggested using very little lecture, putting the most active activities toward the end of class, and engaging students in cooperative learning activities, student presentations, and projects. One teacher emphasized the importance of modeling expectations for students. He brings current events into the curriculum during the first semester and has his students analyze the events and relate them to their lives. By second semester, he finds that his students are raising current events in class. Other ideas included using dramatizations, audio- and videotapes, and starting each day with a quote of the day or a warm-up.

One teacher identified teacher energy in relation to teaching ninth graders in 100-minute periods. This teacher remarked, "Teachers really have to pace themselves, particularly on days when you have no break [planning period]. This is even harder on those who are involved in coaching or other extracurricular activities because, for those teachers, the day is even longer."

Finally, one teacher was opposed to 100-minute periods for ninth graders. This teacher explained, "I think kids are more stressed with the 100-minute periods. I think 100 minutes [periods] result in many failures. If I don't see kids every day, it results in fractures. Kids need to see certain stable relationships every day."

D. Focus Group with Ninth Grade Students—Last Spring

After looking at the results of the ninth grade student surveys, we felt that we would benefit from hearing from the students in a more intimate setting. We ran two focus groups during lunch in early June, with six students in one and seven in the other. Students took their task to advise us on the block periods very seriously, and they put a great deal of thought and reflection into their responses. This student input served to flesh out the feedback we had received on the written surveys from the ninth graders six weeks earlier.

Particularly interesting to us were students' answers to the question: "What is the best thing about 100-minute periods?" with the follow-up question: "What is the worst thing about 100-minute periods?"

The responses were:

Best
Can get in more depth
You have longer to do things
Not getting cut off
Not meeting every day; extra time between meetings to do longer assignments
More time to get stuff done; less homework
An extra day for homework
Getting a break mid-period

Worst

It can be hard to stay awake

You can run out of stuff to do

It can get boring

Tough if you have a short attention span

If you're bored, you might fall asleep

You can have too long to do an activity, so if it's boring, you might just
   avoid doing it

Students thought highly of teachers who used more variety and creativity at the
beginning of the year. Although the focus group was held in June, students re-
membered well which classes had set a tone of stimulation and activity and which
had not. The students urged teachers to make a special effort in the first few class
meetings to capture students' attention and engage them. They seemed to feel that
teachers didn't necessarily have to keep that effort up forever, but that it was extremely critical at the start of the year.

In terms of getting specific ideas about classroom strategies for student success,
the most fruitful question we asked students was: "Think about a class that uses the
100-minute periods well. (Don't name any teacher names!) What does the teacher
do in that class that helps use the 100-minute periods as well as possible?" Students' responses fell into the following categories:

- Breaks
- Variety
- Discussion
- Routine
- Very little unstructured time
- Agenda for the day is on the board

In our Action Plan we address these categories of strategies teachers can use in
their classes to maximize their students' performance.

E. Survey of Eighth Graders—Last Spring

To set a baseline of students' educational attitudes and experiences, we decided to
survey a heterogeneous group of 34 eighth graders from Einstein Middle School.
As anticipated, we received a variety of student opinions on the middle school's
six-period schedule and 50-minute class length.

Five of the 34 students enjoyed the variety that the six-period day schedule offers. Several students felt that it was "easier to pay attention" in 50-minute class
periods and that the "day goes by fast." Some students, however, commented that
50 minutes is often insufficient time for learning. For instance, one student said,

"Teachers run out of time." Another noted, "I have to rush through work," and yet another remarked time is wasted at the beginning and end of the period. Six students found the schedule tiring, confusing, or stressful.

The next set of questions in this survey focused on the types of teaching/learning activities that eighth grade teachers typically used and which activities maintained students' attention best. According to a majority of students, on an average day, eighth grade teachers used mostly lecture and/or independent reading/writing exercises. With regard to their ability to pay attention, students most preferred group work (59 percent) and all group discussion (50 percent). Other activities identified as positive were independent reading/writing (41 percent), hands-on activities (35 percent), and pair work (32 percent). Eighty-four percent of the students agreed that they had the most success in classes with either some or a lot of movement. After tallying these responses, we realized that we should have asked students to rank the activities during which they found themselves best able to pay attention, compared with those their teachers used most often. Because we are interested in maximizing student learning, this comparison would have given us more to reflect on with regard to our own teaching practices.

Finally, we asked for students' ideas about what they and others could do to help them adjust to the 100-minute period schedule at Shorewood the following year. We had dual purposes in asking this question. First, we wanted students to begin to reflect on this issue and prepare themselves mentally for the coming year. Second, we hoped to gather information that would help students in their transition to Shorewood. Responses fell into three categories: what students could do for themselves; what Einstein teachers could do to prepare them better; and what Shorewood ninth grade teachers could do to help them adjust to the new schedule.

Some of the students' ideas for self-preparation included increasing their concentration levels, getting more sleep, reading for longer periods of time, eating better, using more effective time management skills, and talking with current Shorewood students about ninth grade. Students' ideas about what their eighth grade teachers could do included giving them "a lot of tests and writing assignments," and "practicing 100-minute periods" with students. Their advice for teachers at Shorewood was to "have breaks during the period," let them "work with friends," "give [them] time to adjust," and "not [give] too much homework the first few weeks." They also recommended that we "vary activities," use "different teaching styles," and provide "mentors."

Overall, we were impressed by the eighth graders' perceptive comments about their impending transition to 100-minute periods. This survey prompted us to reflect more carefully on our own teaching practices and to find ways to integrate the students' suggestions into our classrooms on a regular basis. Our Action Plan explores ideas about how to help ninth graders in their transition to 100-minute periods.

F. Survey of Shorewood Ninth Grade Students—This Fall

When we surveyed this year's ninth graders about their initial reactions to 100-minute periods, we found several clear trends. There was a strongly positive response to the question, "How do you feel about 100-minute periods?" Sixty-seven percent of the responses (56 of 83) were "love them" or "like them." Thirty percent were neutral. We were surprised to learn that only two students said they didn't like 100-minute periods, and that no students in this sample said that they "hated" them. We found it encouraging that so few students had negative reactions to 100-minute periods.

Given our concern about the problems created when classes meet every other day as opposed to every day, we were surprised that 30 percent of the students noted that having more time between classes for completing their homework was one of their favorite aspects of the schedule. This response suggested to us that we need to look carefully at the differences between students who can manage the ABC structure and those who cannot, and provide quick intervention early in the ninth grade school year for those who are struggling.

Twenty-one students commented that the schedule allowed them the chance to do and learn more. Thirteen students noted that they now had the time to expand their learning in 100-minute periods. Several students noted that 100-minute periods allowed them to carry out longer activities in class without having to break them up over two or more days. Only two students remarked that they couldn't take in so much information in a single class meeting. One student complained that there was "too much homework." These comments, though not offered by the majority of students, do support our sense that 100-minute periods can lend themselves to better learning experiences. We found it exciting that some students, on their own, appreciated 100-minute periods because these longer classes enabled them to learn and accomplish more. A question for us as teachers is, then, how to increase the number of students who share this experience and perception.

Students also gave us strong messages regarding instructional practices within block classes. They made it clear that they don't enjoy sitting too long or doing the same thing the whole period. They suggested that teachers need to limit the length of their lectures and make class more interesting by intentionally creating variety. One student summed it up nicely, saying, "It's [the 100-minute period is] positive only if we do a variety of activities."

One message that came through clearly is that many students believe they need breaks during the 100-minute period. When asked what advice they would give teachers to help them adjust to longer periods, 46 percent of the ninth graders said, "Give breaks." Without breaks, eight students said they found class to be boring and monotonous. We believe that if students are offered effective breaks, they will be able to remain engaged for the entire period. One strategy that we have used with success is to include a four- to five-minute break as part of a transition from one activity to the next, or include a similar break when students hand in, put away, and/or pick up materials. The key to this practice is to keep the break to four- to five-minutes and not let the time expand. It's important to encourage ninth grade students to move their bodies during the break. We have also found it useful to tell students what activities will follow the break so they can be mentally and physically prepared to participate.

Finally, 35 percent of the ninth graders thought 100-minute periods are too long. This large minority underlined for us the importance of incorporating breaks and a variety of activities into each block period to help these students learn to see the longer period as engaging and productive.

Action Plan

After all of our surveying, interviewing, and analyzing, the rewarding time has finally come—putting into practice the strategies that can aid ninth graders in their transition to 100-minute periods. Over and over, and in many different ways, students told us that they need a variety of activities to keep their attention and make learning meaningful. At the same time, they appreciate the predictability and routine that well-structured periods provide. How does one merge these seemingly competing needs? We recommend to other teachers and have begun to develop or reinforce in our own classrooms the following strategies:

Post the daily agenda on the board, and, when possible, share weekly, biweekly, or even monthly class calendars with students, and review these agendas and calendars with students. Giving this information to students and drawing their attention to it provides them with an overview of how time will be spent in class, nurtures their cognitive development as they learn to think about managing time in new ways, and helps to support their development of time management skills. It also gives students a global overview of their own learning, thereby minimizing the sense of disconnection or fractionalization that some students experience in school. Students must be provided with this cognitive scaffolding on which to hang their understanding of the learning goals of the course.

Give students enough opportunities to move their bodies in each block period. Ninth graders need movement. If planned purposefully, the transitions between activities can provide this. Teachers can also use teaching/learning activities that incorporate movement, such as small groups, drama, simulations, labs, student board work, values lines, charades, student presentations, learning stations, and scavenger hunts.

Include a variety of teaching/learning activities within each block period. Students told us repeatedly that the teachers who use 100-minute periods most effectively offer a variety of activities in each class meeting.

Use discussions, both small- and large-group. Discussion was strongly recommended by students, because it allows them to engage with one another, process concepts, and reflect on and personalize new learning.

Provide purposeful, well-structured breaks. Students called for regular breaks as an essential part of life within the 100-minute period schedule. Rather than perceiving a break as losing five minutes of class, breaks should be seen as an integrated part of the learning experience. Breaks can be linked to picking up or handing in materials to be used for the activity following the break (i.e., handouts, atlases, tangible objects). Movement out of their seats offers a mental recharge to some students and a kinesthetic outlet to others. For example, after students have read about religious traditions in China and worked with a partner to identify key ideas from their reading, discussed these ideas, and noted them on a chart, the teacher might call for a five-minute break. The teacher could announce that before the end of this five-minute period, students need to come to the front of the room and pick up the next set of readings, then seat themselves in groups of four.

Teach time management skills. The teachers from Einstein Middle School suggested that we give new ninth graders some sort of visual aid showing how one 100-minute period is equal to two 50-minute periods. We need to make what is implicit to teachers explicit for students. To be most effective, sharing such visual aids should be combined with a discussion about how the 100-minute period and the ABC schedule affect homework load, effective use of time, organizational strategies, and long-term planning.

As with most high schools across the country, our high school has experienced a high failure rate for ninth graders. Many of our students admit that time management plays a major role in this failure, and that procrastination is a problem in their academic lives. Therefore, teachers of ninth graders, and particularly in a 100-minute block period ABC schedule, need to incorporate appropriate instruction in time management and planning skills within their course curricula. We need to identify student weaknesses in this area in September and address them with specific instruction.

Teach organizational skills and expect organization from students. Teachers from both Einstein and Shorewood recommended that we overtly teach students organizational skills and that we gradually expect more and more of them in this area. We need to identify clear expectations and standards for organization in our classes, and we need to provide students with models and appropriately scaffolded instruction in developing their own organizational skills. For example, students could examine a model student notebook from the previous year. A few days before the first notebook/learning log check of the year, the teacher could provide students with a cover sheet that lists each assignment due and in what order the notebook should be compiled. (Of course all assignments would have been explained and assigned already.) The next time the notebook was to be reviewed, the teacher could tell students a few days in advance when notebooks would be due, but not give the cover sheet until the beginning of the class session, asking that notebooks be handed in by the end of break time. Gradually upping expectations can be appropriate and effective as long as one gives clear guidelines about each phase and provides needed modeling and instruction.

Establish and maintain stable relationships with students. One of the ninth grade teachers from our focus group explained that it is essential to create a climate of stability in the teacher/student relationship, particularly when classes only meet three times a week. Teachers of ninth graders need to focus their energies as much as they can on using the longer period to facilitate the development of relationships with their students, particularly as they use lecture less as a teaching/learning method and devote more time to interacting with individuals and small groups as a coach.

One of our colleagues who was very concerned about ninth grade success has addressed this by establishing a *Big Brother/Big Sister Program* in his own classroom (as noted above). For each ninth grade class he teaches, he has one upperclass female and one upperclass male student who participate as aides. "I have no illusion that I'm hip," quipped the teacher. The *big brother* and *big sister* are hip and personable and they build strong relationships with the students. This program changes the "adult" to ninth grader ratio from 1:30 to 3:30. This teacher has piloted this program successfully for several years in his own classroom, and this approach will be tried by 15 teachers next year. These teachers will collaborate in this project, and the mentoring students will be tied into a broader program that aims to teach pedagogical skills to youth.

Conclusion

As we conducted our study, we learned the most from *listening to the ninth grade student voice*. It has been so valuable to us—in our day-to-day planning, the structuring of our projects, and the adjustment of some instructional practices—that we feel it is surely of similar value to others searching for ways to best reach ninth graders and assist in their transition to high school and 100-minute periods. Our next step is to share what we've learned through this study to help develop a more cohesive plan for ninth grade success in our own school.

One unexpected outcome of our research was the high level of satisfaction with the 100-minute period schedule expressed by this year's ninth grade class. Their adaptability and the thoughtfulness of their responses in surveys early this fall were considerably stronger than last year's. This improvement led us to wonder if the fact that we'd surveyed this same group of students as eighth graders the previous spring had an impact on their experience and perceptions. Our hunch now is that the reflection and predicting about 100-minute periods that we asked them to do last spring gave many of these students an opportunity to prepare mentally for the transition to the high school schedule. Also, completing our survey in early fall likely encouraged many of these students to reflect on how they were doing with the new schedule at that point and helped them to make needed adjustments. We suggest repeating this process each spring with eighth graders at Einstein and then at Shorewood in the early fall once their ninth grade year is in full swing.

Appendix A

Transition from 50 to 100-Minute Periods
Shorewood Ninth Graders—Last Spring

1. How do you feel about 100-minute periods? (circle one)

   Love it   Like it   Neutral   50 min. is better   Hate it

2. Why?

3. Circle the activities your teachers use on an average day:

   Independent reading/writing   Hands-on activities

   Group work   Learning games

   Viewing videos   All group discussion

   Teacher lecture   Student presentations

   Research   Note taking

   Other (please list):

4. What is the best thing about 100-minute periods?

5. What is the worst thing about 100-minute periods?

6. If you could change 100-minutes periods, what would you do? Why?

7. Of the 100 minutes, how many minutes do you spend:

    _____ Daydreaming or feeling lost or confused?

    _____ Listening to the teacher or other students?

    _____ Doodling, writing notes, doing work for another class?

    _____ Working on the assigned activity (as an individual or in groups)?

    _____ Chatting?

8. Pick two of your classes, one that you think uses the 100 minutes effectively and one that you feel doesn't use the 100 minutes effectively. **Do not tell us the names of the teachers.** Tell us about the structure of these classes.

    More effective class for you   *Less effective class for you*

    Beginning: Beginning:

Middle: Middle:

End: End:

Further comments about why this   Further comments about why this
class works for you: class doesn't work for you:

9. When you first came to Shorewood, what was difficult about 100-minute
   periods?

10. Is this still difficult for you? Why or why not?

11. What advice would you give to a new ninth grader about dealing with 100-minute periods?

12. How can teachers help students adjust to 100-minute periods?

13. What suggestions would you make to your teachers about how they could use the 100-minute periods better?

Appendix B

Focus Group Questions—Eighth Grade Teachers

What do you feel are the advantages and disadvantages of the 6-period per day, 50-minute period schedule?

What perceptions do you think kids have of that schedule?

During the WASL (Washington Assessment of Student Learning) administration, how did kids respond to the 100-minute periods? (Follow up: How was your planning affected?)

What predictions can you make about how your students will adjust to 100-minute periods?

What kind of students do you think will have the most trouble with the adjustment?

What advice would you give ninth grade teachers about how to ease the transition for these incoming ninth graders, particularly with respect to 100-minute periods?

Appendix C

Focus Group Questions—Ninth Grade Teachers

What are some of the critical issues facing ninth graders in their transition to high school (and, specifically, to 100-minute periods)?

How much of a role do you see 100-minute periods playing in ninth graders' success (or lack thereof)?

What kind of comments have ninth graders made since the fall about having 100-minute classes?

What strategies do you use to help ninth graders adjust to high school, and Shorewood in general?

Have you taken any steps specifically to help ninth graders adjust to the 100-minute period?

On a typical day, how do you break up the 100-minute period? What sorts of activities do you use regularly? What have you found works best in terms of the order of activities within 100-minute periods?

In your perception, what use of the 100-minute period do you find keeps the most kids on task?

Do you feel there is anything that eighth grade teachers or Einstein could do to prepare kids for the 100-minute periods before they get to Shorewood?

Appendix D

Questions for Ninth Grade Focus Group

Prior to asking the following questions, remind students that the questions are similar to those on the written questionnaire they completed in May. Please let them know that we are hoping to explore these questions further in the focus group to better enable us to make concrete changes and suggestions regarding the best use of 100-minute periods. Thanks!

1. What is the best thing about 100-minute periods? (Follow up: What is the worst thing about 100-minute periods?)

2. What specific things did your teachers do to help you adjust to 100-minute periods at the beginning of the year? (Follow up: What specific things could your teachers have done that might have helped you adjust to the 100-minute periods more easily?)

3. Think about a class that uses the 100-minute periods well. (Don't name any teacher names!) What does the teacher do in that class that helps use the 100-minute periods effectively?

4. Take a moment to think about the kind of student you were last year and your feelings toward school. Now think about whether that has changed this year. If you feel your attitudes toward school and yourself as a student have changed, what do you see as the causes of that change? Does the 100-minute period have anything to do with the change?

5. What advice would you give incoming ninth graders about adjusting to 100-minute periods?

Appendix E

Student Survey

Thank you for taking the time to thoughtfully complete this survey.
Your opinion matters!

Eighth Graders, Spring, Einstein Middle School

Take a moment to reflect on your current Einstein schedule and your elementary school schedule. Think ahead to the 100-minute schedule at Shorewood. Remember for a moment the different schedule you recently had for the WASL testing days.

1. What is your opinion on having six class periods every day?

2. How do you feel about class periods being 50 minutes in length?

3. Circle activities that your teachers use on an *average* day:

   independent reading/writing   hands-on activities   doing research
   group work   learning games   taking notes
   viewing videos   all group discussion   pair work
   student presentations   teacher lecture

   OTHER (please list):

4. Think of a normal day in a typical class; how many of the different activities above do your teachers ask you to do in one period?

   1   2   3   4   5   6   7

5. In which of these activities do you find yourself paying attention best?

   1. _____
   2. _____
   3. _____

6. Which three of the activities mentioned in question 3 do your teachers use the most?

   1. _____
   2. _____
   3. _____

7. What things do you think will be better with 100-minute periods, and what do you think will be worse, if anything?

   BETTER   SAME   WORSE

8. Of the 50 minutes in a class period, how many minutes do you spend:

   _____ Daydreaming or feeling lost or confused?
   _____ Listening to the teacher or other students?
   _____ Doodling, writing notes; doing work for another class?
   _____ Working on the assigned activity (as an individual or in groups)?
   _____ Chatting?

9. Do you have the most success in classes where you have:
   (Please circle the situation that's best for you)

little to no movement	*some movement*	*a lot of movement*
you're in your same seat all period	there are some seat transitions or out of seat time, but not a lot	you move around a lot, you're often up changing seats or doing activities away from your seat

10. How many of your six classes have:

Little to no movement	*some movement*	*a lot of movement*
_____ classes	_____ classes	_____ classes

11. What are some things that you could be doing (or people could be doing with you) to help you adjust to the 100-minute periods at Shorewood next year?

Appendix F

Student Survey on 100-Minute Periods
Ninth Graders, Early Fall, Shorewood High School

Dear ninth grader,

We're very interested in your *initial* reaction to 100-minute periods. We'd like to ask you a few questions about how you're getting used to them. Please take a few minutes to think about and respond in detail to each of the following questions. Thank you in advance for your helpful input!

1. How do you feel about 100-minute periods? (circle one)

   Love them   Like them   Neutral   50 min. is better   Hate them

2. In what way have they affected your learning—positively or negatively? Why?

3. What is the best thing about 100-minute periods?

4. What is the worst thing about 100-minute periods?

5. What advice would you give your teachers to help you get used to 100-minute periods?

2

Teaching Ninth Graders in the Block Schedule: A Search for Better Instructional Practices

Toni Roberts
Shorewood High School

Toni Roberts, a high school science teacher, wanted to study how a series of related innovations in curriculum, classroom practices and organizational structures, and teaching/learning activities would affect the learning and achievement of the ninth grade students in her Integrated Physical Science classes. Using action research practices for her study, she found that implementing clear and consistent classroom routines, a thematic and inquiry-based curriculum, focused uses of student notebooks for scheduling and completed work, and regular use of conceptual maps, as well as several other practices, demonstrated significant positive results for student learning and achievement. She also identified how she could use the 100-minute block period effectively to keep students active and engaged and to encourage their learning and accomplishment.

Introduction

After four years of teaching ninth graders in the block schedule, I am still searching for better instructional practices that meet the interest, maturity, and developmental needs of my students. My greatest frustration as a high school teacher has been the generally low academic achievement of ninth graders. In conversations with colleagues in my science department and across disciplines, it has become apparent that this is a systemic problem within our school. Thus, it was my goal to experiment with curriculum, classroom design and management, and instructional strategies in hopes of promoting better academic success among my ninth grade science students.

In addition to other classes, I teach ninth grade Integrated Physical Science at Shorewood High School (described in chapter 1) in Shoreline, Washington, just north of Seattle. Shorewood has one feeder middle school that operates on trimesters and does *not* require full years of science. The science background with which our freshmen enter is inconsistent because students are blocked in middle school and receive a different science emphasis depending on which block they're enrolled in. Thus, our ninth graders come into our science program with varied science experiences.

Historically, our school has required two years of laboratory science for graduation. For most students, the first year occurs in ninth grade, when they take physical science. The second year is sophomore biology. Students cannot progress to biology until they pass physical science, so if they fail ninth grade science, they repeat it in tenth grade. We have phased out all credit recovery science classes.

Seven years ago, with a shift in our department's personnel, our ninth grade program was changed to Integrated Physical Science with an infusion of the earth sciences into foundational physical science principles. The department had a basic physical science textbook that was below grade level (seventh–eighth grade). To accommodate integration of earth science topics, the department purchased an above-grade-level textbook that surveys the earth science fields (eleventh–twelfth grade). The ninth grade program used these two textbooks to teach students physical science principles while studying earth science topics.

When I began teaching the course four years ago, three of my colleagues also taught it. We all worked independently, which was the school norm when I arrived, so it was up to each teacher to determine the scope and sequence of course content. During this first year I stayed one topic ahead of my students, learning the content myself and scrapping to find activities to support the content. The majority of the teacher resources supporting our two texts had long since disappeared, and my colleagues' lesson plans were housed in their heads and, thus, largely unavailable. I spent many weekend hours at Seattle Pacific University's library, copying activities from periodicals such as *The Science Teacher*, *Science Scope*, and *The Physics Teacher*. I also invested substantial personal funds to purchase science curriculum I found through the National Science Teacher's Association's curriculum catalogue. I did the best I could. I delivered content through direct instruction, showed the occasional Bill Nye science video from public television, supported my lectures with activities that I either created or found, and gave virtually no homework. I survived.

The second year teaching this course involved a lot of reflection on my part. I now knew my content. But how could I make the class more student-centered, inquiry-based, and project oriented? So I focused and refined my course's content, tried new activities and projects, and experimented with different ways of managing student work. Still, I was frustrated by my role as the primary content giver and by my students' low achievement. It was clear to me that they needed more than just me to learn the science, and I needed more than just me to feel good about what I was doing as a teacher.

This brings me to my third and fourth years teaching this course and implementation of this action research project. I could summarize my third year with Essential Academic Learning Requirements (EALR), the legislatively mandated Washington State academic standards. My entire first semester was spent stressing about all of the content I was not covering. How can I possibly cover all of that content in one year? I cannot reinvent the wheel, nor should I. There must be curriculum out there that can do a better job of teaching science content and process than I was. So I contacted every publisher I could and had boxes of curriculum sent to me.

It took nearly a semester, but I convinced all of my ninth grade science colleagues to study new curriculum options. And what a process this was. It was difficult for us to agree on what content should be taught and at what depth, even with the EALR as our guiding beacon. It was even more difficult for us to agree on the type of curriculum we wanted and thought was good for kids. We had all worked so hard to develop our own programs from scratch that it was very difficult to open our minds to other curricular options. We did agree, however, that with the increase in ninth grade enrollment and the need for more teachers to teach the course, it was imperative that we have an articulated curriculum that could serve as a unifying structure for all of us. It had to be more than our two current textbooks, neither of which was age appropriate, and neither of which we had enough of to issue to students.

We divided the curriculum we were examining into two groups: textbooks that integrated large themes, and smaller modules that integrated similar but more specific themes. The problem with integrated curriculum, we found, was that it integrates all fields of science: biology, physical, and earth. Sounds great, except that we had just instituted an expensive new biology program the year before. Thus, if we purchased integrated textbooks, we felt we would have a hard time teaching the content while removing the biology. We did find that with modules, we could select certain topics that had a larger focus on the earth and physical sciences and did not usurp the sophomore biology curriculum. But my colleagues still could not imagine themselves teaching our current program in such a different, totally integrated way.

I decided to act as the test subject for the group and to pilot a particular integrated, inquiry-based, modular curriculum for one full quarter, with this underlying purpose: to examine the effect this curriculum and a change in teaching to accommodate this curriculum would have on ninth grade success. I did in fact pilot two modules during the fourth quarter of my third year teaching this course. Based on my success with two pilot classes, we purchased the program for all ninth grade science students starting with the freshmen entering this fall. I am currently teaching the program this year to three ninth grade classes. This study details my experiences with changing my instructional practices to accommodate this program and to better meet the needs of ninth graders. This research was conducted with two classes last spring and three classes this fall.

Underlying Observations and Assumptions

This research was prompted by several observations and assumptions I had made over the first three years of teaching our science program to ninth graders in the block schedule at Shorewood High School.

Observations

1. Most ninth grade students are inherently disorganized.
2. Students at Shorewood enter the ninth grade with varied science experiences, skills, and knowledge.
3. In the block schedule, classes meet every other day. Ninth grade students have difficulty remembering course concepts and assignments from one class meeting to the next, given the intervening day for distraction.
4. Many or most ninth grade students find it challenging to pay attention to complex content for 100 minutes.
5. Ninth graders respond well to routines.
6. Ninth graders need more opportunities to learn content than direct instruction and classroom-based elaboration activities alone can offer.
7. Ninth graders generally have a difficult time adjusting to the fact that grades now count in high school, compared with middle school, where they could fail all of their classes and still be promoted.

Assumptions

1. Curriculum can have a profound effect on student academic achievement and attitude. Our department's lack of a clear, accessible, age-appropriate curricular program was a contributing factor to the low academic success of many of my students.
2. The 100-minute, ABC schedule poses special problems for ninth graders including long class periods in one room and classes meeting only every other day. Thus, the ABC schedule may also be an initial contributing factor in the low academic success of many of my students. Additionally, instruction that does not use and accommodate this schedule effectively can lead to less academic success for students.
3. My inability to develop consistent classroom routines and clear expectations for student work because of an irregular, incongruous curriculum and lack of experience with teaching the course was probably also a contributing factor to the low academic success of many of my students.

Research Questions

Based on my assumptions about our program and schedule, and on the observations I had made in my classroom regarding ninth grade student achievement, attitudes, and behavior, I focused my research on the following questions:

1. How can an inquiry-based, thematic, integrated, and modular curriculum affect ninth grade student achievement?
2. How can the development of clear and consistent classroom routines affect the achievement of my ninth grade science students in 100-minute block period classes?
3. How can the use of concept maps and vocabulary development based on learning Latin and Greek roots promote academic achievement?
4. How can the way student work is managed in my classroom affect student achievement?

Teaching/Learning Practices

I already knew a lot about what did not work well with my ninth graders. I wanted to use this action research study to investigate the efficacy of a new set of teaching/learning practices to which my experience and reflection had led me. These were:

1. *Use the modules as the basis of the ninth grade Integrated Physical Science curriculum*, keeping true to the design and intent of the curriculum without adding or substituting other, more comfortable activities. Each student was issued a module and was required to bring the module to class daily and to take it home for use with homework.

   In the spring of last year, the following modules were piloted: *Current Thoughts* (electricity, magnetism, and the nervous system) and *Turn Left at Alpha Centauri* (space and stellar astronomy). In the fall of this school year, these modules served as the basis for the curriculum, *Wildfire* (the chemistry, ecology, and thermodynamics of fire), *Quake, Bake, and Shake* (plate tectonics, earthquakes, volcanoes); and *Going for Gold* (mineral, gem, rock formation and properties). (All modules are published by the Everyday Learning Co.)

   Each module follows a similar structure. Introductory reading introduces a theme and asks basic questions of the student. For example, in *Wildfire*, the students are asked questions such as: What causes fire? Why are fires hot and bright? Why does fanning a fire make it burn better, while smothering a fire extinguishes it? When a forest burns, where does all of the material from the tree go? Why do scientists intentionally start forest fires? How does the landscape recover from a forest fire? Students then discuss their responses to these questions. I had students take notes on this discussion, titling the first page in their notebook: *What Do You Know about Fire?* After this discussion, designed to ignite student interest in the topic and illuminate students' prior knowledge, students jump into an introductory inquiry lab activity. When they have completed the lab activity, they write responses to a handful of analysis questions. For homework, they read a short passage (one–three pages) that introduces the scientific concepts behind the investigation they conducted in class and answer a few more analysis questions at the application/critical thinking level of Bloom's Taxonomy.

Each module is organized into three or four sections, with each section containing three to six inquiry investigations. Each investigation poses a question, provides a hands-on activity to explore the question being asked, and then provides a short content acquisition reading allowing the student to learn the scientific principles behind the investigation. At the end of each section is a "Section Wrap-Up" reading that ties together all of the activities and readings in the section and applies it to the larger theme. In *Wildfire*, the module was organized into the following sections: *Firestorm* (the chemistry of fire), *On The Fire Line* (the thermodynamics and chemistry of how fires spread and are prevented), and *Out of the Ashes* (the ecology of how the landscape recovers from fire). Then, at the end of the module, a "Module Wrap-Up" reading reviews all of the concepts introduced in the module and summarizes how the concepts all relate to the theme.

2. *Use an assignment log to help students manage their work.* Every class period, students date and write the activities for the day in their assignment log to give an overview of the day's agenda and a record of the work to be collected. This also gives parents a means for monitoring student homework and work completion.

3. *Manage student work by means of a module notebook.* Each module lasts from three to five weeks, depending on the topic. Students bring a three-ring binder to class every day, dedicated solely to science. In the binder are their module (thin enough to be hole-punched into their binder), their assignment log, and their work in order from the first day of the module to the last. At the end of the module, students then staple all of their work in order behind the assignment log and turn it in for evaluation. I also experimented with students developing notebook covers that illustrate the content they have learned in the unit, to which they stapled their work.

4. *Use concept mapping as a means for showing connections between activities conducted in class and concepts learned.* As the unit progresses, students and I build a concept map together that relates each activity and concept to the larger theme.

5. *Focus on Latin and Greek roots encountered in the module readings and other course content to help students develop a richer vocabulary.* As part of their module notebook, students maintain a Latin and Greek root page. For each investigation conducted, I identify words that contain basic roots. As a class, the students and I then dissect the roots and identify their meanings. Students are then tested periodically on their memory and application of these root words.

6. *Develop and adhere to a set of basic classroom routines on which students can rely, and use these routines to establish a pattern of classroom behavior and expectation.* I implemented the following generalized routine as a result of the pattern of content delivery the modules established, my desire to help students develop strong and reliable work habits and deeper conceptual understanding of course content, and the need to better accommodate the special opportunities and challenges that result from block scheduling:

a. As students walk into the room, I have an entry activity that I call a *warm-up* on the overhead. These entry tasks usually involve three or more questions that review the previous day's work or help students to focus on or clarify important concepts. Students pick up a quarter-sheet of scratch paper that I keep in the front of the room, write their name on the paper, and answer the questions. During this time, I take attendance and go around the room making contact with each student and stamping her/his homework. I then collect the warm-ups, and with a quick glance, can identify the concepts students understand and those with which they are having difficulty. This generally takes around 10 to 15 minutes.

   I find this time invaluable for several reasons. First, it helps students to focus on a class they have not been in for two days. Second, it helps students review and practice course content. Third, I have the chance to make contact with all of the students in the class, asking how they are and checking on their progress with work completion and responses to the warm-up questions. Fourth, it allows me to award points for class participation. Warm-ups are worth up to five points a day, depending on the quality of the responses, for a total of 10 percent of the student's grade.

b. After warm-ups have been collected, I ask students to take out their assignment logs. I write down the activities for the day on the overhead, and students copy this into their assignment log. This allows me to communicate very clearly to students both the agenda for the day and the work that will be required and collected for evaluation. It also gives students a reliable place to check for homework, and it gives parents a means for monitoring their student's progress and work completion.

c. I then spend about 15 to 20 minutes in direct instruction, which is mostly a review and elaboration of the previous day's activity and reading. Since students experienced the concept firsthand with an inquiry activity, had to answer some very analytical questions, and did a short reading for conceptual understanding on their own at home, this takes the form of a review rather than a lecture. I ask students to title a piece of paper "Investigation (1) Discussion" and to write as I write on the overhead. I also employ visual organizers of various types that I hand out to students to develop as we discuss the content at hand. This discussion allows me to find out what students are learning and to clarify and elaborate on important concepts. We also use this time to discuss the warm-up and homework questions. I commonly find that students go back and edit their answers to the homework after these discussions.

d. Students are asked next to take out their module concept map and Latin and Greek root page. We spend no more than 10 minutes adding the concept we just discussed to the concept map and deriving the roots from words encountered in the reading and discussion. I have found that students who are predominantly visual learners respond well to the use of concept maps to illuminate connections between content, and that students who are quite verbally adept experience great success with the use of Latin and Greek roots to develop scientific vocabulary.

e. At this point in the 100-minute class period, approximately 50 minutes remain for students to engage in a hands-on inquiry activity. As part of their homework the previous night, students were required to read the lab activity in their module and compose an objective, set-up, and data table for the lab. My role is to facilitate students' work as they conduct the experiment. As the course progresses, students become more skilled at using this time constructively and becoming self-directed learners. For most activities, students are able to conduct the inquiry, collect data, clean up and return materials, and answer analysis questions posed by the module within this time frame.

I used this structure as the pattern for most of my 100-minute periods, although at times I modified the structure to fit the nature of a particular module. Some investigations required long-term sampling, others involved research, and still others involved viewing videos and other media. Even with some variation in this structure, students came to know it and to expect its various elements.

Research Methodology

At first this research was intended to be an investigation of the pilot of two modules with my fourth-quarter students last spring. But then our department actually purchased the program for use by all ninth grade students, and I continued my research with three classes this fall. So this study focuses on two different groups of students. The methods by which I collected information changed from the first group to the second, even though I experimented with nearly identical instructional practices each time. The data I collected from my research were obtained from four sources: pre and post student questionnaires, student focus groups, personal journaling about my experiences, and artifacts of student learning and work completion.

The students who served as the pilot group for these modules were accustomed to a completely different mode of instruction. All of the content delivery came from me, with the exception of several research projects, and they had done literally no homework on a regular basis. I also had not used concept mapping or Latin and Greek root development with these students. And all of the labs they had conducted had been traditional, "prove the scientific principle is true" type of investigations that are readily available in most curriculum sources. The only true classroom routine to which they were accustomed was warm-ups. So this change in instructional practice, class routine, and standards for classroom work and homework was quite dramatic, and it came in the last eight weeks of school. As a result, the data I collected from the students were not as telling as my own professional opinion of the impact and potential of these changes.

These students were asked if they were willing to participate in a pilot of a new curriculum that the department was considering purchasing for all ninth graders. They seemed willing, not knowing that homework would be required of them. I administered a prequestionnaire to these two classes asking them about their experiences in my class and if they thought certain specific changes would affect their learning and achievement (see appendix A). I then introduced my set of new teaching/learning practices and made journal reflections of my observations. At about the fifth week of the pilot, I conducted a focus group with six students who served as a representative sample of my class population and asked them to discuss their thoughts about the modules, the routines I established in the class, the use of concept maps and Latin and Greek roots for vocabulary development, the use of the assignment log, and the way class work was managed in module notebooks. Near the end of the pilot, I administered a postquestionnaire to the two classes (see appendix B).

With my classes this fall I have mostly collected data from my observations of student learning, achievement, and attitudes. These students started with the modules and instructional practices I established to teach effectively with these modules from the first day of school. Thus, I have not administered questionnaires to them. But I have looked at artifacts of student achievement, such as work completion rates, and compared these to those demonstrated by the pilot group of students, acknowledging that I am comparing two different groups of students, and certain difficulties arise with such a comparison.

Findings and Discussion

1. Use of Inquiry-Based, Thematic, Integrated Modules

As a result of this action research, I am absolutely convinced that curriculum is as critical to student learning and achievement as instructional practice. The use of thematic, integrated modules not only has infused zeal into my teaching of science, it has made my students interested and enthusiastic. As students noted in the pilot focus group and on the postquestionnaire after completing the *Current Thoughts* module: "It's better than before. Different and more interesting, so I stick with it." "The readings are so interesting. They made me think about things in ways I've never thought before." "I'm learning real stuff . . . stuff that you can actually use in everyday life." I am convinced that the framing of scientific content in an integrated, thematic manner gives students an existing mental framework on which to hang new knowledge. What they are learning is suddenly not so nebulous and obscure, and they find enjoyment in learning something that they really can understand. I also noticed that, in discussions, students were better able to explain concepts in their own words and draw parallels to other common phenomena rather than simply paraphrasing what they had read or heard me say.

A second attribute of the modules, aside from presenting material in an interesting, contextual manner, is the instructional approach the curriculum takes: inquiry investigations followed by short content acquisition readings. I was very pleased with the transition of my role from primary content giver to learning facilitator. I personally felt more confident in my teaching knowing that students had more opportunities to learn the scientific concepts than just taking notes from my lectures. Suddenly I found the students asking for my explanations and clarifications on labs and readings, rather than being subjected to them unwillingly. When the pilot students were asked on the prequestionnaire about their greatest difficulty in science class, students reported: "lecture notes," "absorbing information," "remembering information," "concentrating when I don't understand," "understanding the information well enough to be tested on it," and "understanding and interpreting what we've learned." But when I asked the focus group representing these students about taking notes and learning concepts while using the modules, their responses changed to: "I like reading about something first and then having you explain and review it," "I like not having to take so many notes," and "I had an easier time learning the stuff . . . I can't explain why."

I was also very interested in the general response of the students to the modules as curriculum, so on the postquestionnaire I asked them: What do you like and/or dislike about the use of modules in science class? The following comments are representative of the student responses I received:

Module Size and Use
- "I like working out of the module instead of a big book I have to carry around."
- "They're less messy and confusing than always getting handouts."
- "They were fun."
- "They made it easy to learn."
- "What I really like was how small they were. Most days I pick only one or two books to bring to school, but this book I can bring every day."
- "I like how the book is small and has so many pictures and interesting facts."
- "The modules helped me to learn more."

Module Organization

- "It's easy to tell what chapter we're going to be doing next."
- "They're small and we always know what we'll be doing in class."
- "I like that we don't have to carry around a huge book and I can look in the module to see what we're doing the next day."
- "It's easy to follow."
- "I like knowing what to expect."
- "I like how it is split into interesting units."

Investigations

- "I look forward to doing the labs."
- "The experiments were fun."
- "I like that the labs were easy to follow and understand."
- "I don't like that if you do something wrong, you don't know it until the next day."
- "I don't like to read so many steps in the labs."

Readings

- "They help me understand what I'm doing."
- "I liked how the readings were short but really straightforward and detailed."
- "I didn't like that you couldn't just skim the reading for answers to the questions, but that you had to actually think."
- "I don't like answering all of the questions."

Perhaps the most significant data I received from the students about the use of these modules was obtained from the pre- and postquestionnaires. The students were asked on the prequestionnaire if they thought that using the modules would improve their learning. The students responded as follows: 37 percent yes, 6 percent no, and 57 percent maybe. But on the postquestionnaires, after using two modules over an eight-week period, the students responded to the same question as follows: 66 percent yes, 4 percent no, and 30 percent maybe. The students were also asked if using the modules would help them to keep up with daily work and make-up work when they were absent. The prequestionnaire yielded: 45 percent yes, 12.5 percent no, 42.5 percent maybe; the postquestionnaire yielded: 63.5 percent yes, 5 percent no, and 31.5 percent maybe. When asked if using the modules would help them to better understand labs and extract meaning from activities, the students responded on the prequestionnaire: 41 percent yes, 13.5 percent no, 45.5 percent maybe; and on the postquestionnaire: 57 percent yes, 10 percent no, and 33 percent maybe.

Overall, students reported positive feelings about the modules as curriculum and about their use in class. I was impressed with the amount of content the modules were able to teach with relatively little explanation. By applying ideas to a specific theme, the modules were able to explain concepts adequately without needing pages of detail. I rarely felt the need to add more content, detail, or examples. The analysis questions were quite skilled at asking students to apply the information to new situations. With practice, the students became more comfortable with thinking analytically and critically.

2. Development of Clear and Consistent Classroom Routines in 100-Minute Block Periods

The modules' design necessitated my developing a basic pattern in my 100-minute class consisting of students conducting an inquiry investigation, reading about the scientific principle at home, answering questions, and then coming back to school and discussing the material with me and each other. This pattern has allowed me to infuse other routines into each period, such as warm-ups, stamping homework, and using an assignment log.

In addition to adopting the modules themselves, I feel that developing clear and consistent routines was my most significant innovation. As discussed earlier, the warm-ups afforded me the opportunity to track students' conceptual progress, make daily personal contact with students, and monitor their work completion. Each homework reading had a point value attached to it. I stamped the homework to give credit for completion and thoroughness. Each stamp was worth up to five points, separate from the point value for actually answering the questions. Thus, if students did not attempt or complete a homework reading, they would miss the point value associated with the on-time stamp, but could still do the assignment and receive some credit. I found that this gave students fewer excuses for not doing homework. I circulated around the room, making notations in my grade book as to who had and had not completed homework. I could then require these students to come in during our daily 25-minute tutorial period to complete the assignment. Soon students were completing assignments with greater frequency so they didn't have to give up their tutorial period for this.

The assignment log has also proven to be invaluable. Students maintain their own dated record of assignments, and I update it on the overhead every day with the class. In this way, students have no excuse for not knowing what work is required of them. I also send an explanation of all of these routines home to parents at the beginning of the year so that they know they can monitor their child's progress by checking the assignment log. This alone has reduced the number of parent phone calls I receive and parent conferences that are scheduled after the grading period ends. When our special education department's study skills class requests weekly updates of required student work, I simply photocopy the assignment log. Perhaps the greatest benefit I have seen from using the assignment log has been with student absences. When they're absent, students know they must copy the work they missed from the assignment log and make it up. They can get a stamp on their homework the next class session. I no longer have to spend five minutes with each student who missed a class.

On the postquestionnaires and in the focus groups, students offered the following comments about the routines established in class to teach these modules in the 100-minute block schedule:

Warm-Ups and Homework Stamps

- "I like the review time."
- "I like that you talk to me every day."
- "It helps me to remember what we did last class."
- "I like that it's easy points."
- "The homework stamp makes me do it when I'm supposed to."

Assignment Log

- "The assignment sheet keeps me organized."
- "It's easy to catch up on homework when you're sick."
- "I like having this calendar so that everyone knows what to expect."
- "I like knowing exactly what to keep."
- "It helps to know what to pay attention to."

General Class Routines

- "I like knowing what to expect every day."
- "I think it makes the class go by faster."
- "Having to preread the labs and write an objective helps me to understand the labs better."
- "I like that we review a lot, because the more time we spend reviewing, the more I understand."
- "Class is very monotonous."
- "When we do the same thing every day, it gets very old after a while."
- "Fewer labs would be better, they're time-consuming."
- "There are too many labs."
- "I don't like that we're busy all the time."

The pre- and postquestionnaires yielded other interesting data from the students. When asked on the prequestionnaire if they felt they knew what to expect when they came to class, the students responded: 8.5 percent definitely no, 31.5 percent sometimes, 52 percent usually, and 8 percent definitely yes. But on the postquestionnaire, after engaging for eight weeks in the routines that I established, the students responded: 6.5 percent definitely no, 17.5 percent sometimes, 36 percent usually, and 40 percent definitely yes.

Although students did report an element of redundancy in the structure of the class, students in the focus groups explained that they felt "the routines helped to break up the long periods better" and that "this has been my least boring science class ever." The students also reported definitely feeling "forced to be organized in class—which is a good thing." I believe that these routines make success in the class as accessible to everyone as possible. Perhaps the most profound effect that developing such routines has had on the achievement of my students is that it has placed the onus of success strongly on their shoulders. Expectations are clear and consistent, and material is introduced, experienced, and elaborated on in a variety of ways. Opportunities exist for making up incomplete work, and students are reminded by me daily of work that is incomplete or missing.

3. Use of Concept Maps and Latin and Greek Roots

I am a strongly visual learner. Thus I use concept mapping naturally to see how ideas are connected. With adoption of these modules, I found it imperative to use concept mapping as a means for showing my students how the scientific principles they were learning with each investigation related to the module's theme, and that every learning activity we did had a specific purpose. Because the learning activities focused on specific concepts, students could easily lose sight of the larger idea or theme. So I constructed a module concept map with the students during each unit of study. I also had students construct their own concept maps for smaller, more specific concepts with words that I suggested. Students found it difficult at first to construct these maps, even with the aid of selected vocabulary. But with my modeling of mapping skills and periodic practice on their own, students became more adept at building thoughtful connections among the concepts they were learning.

On the whole, student response to the use of concept mapping was positive. Most liked doing a large map for each unit. Students frequently asked me, "Are we going to work on the concept map today?" They used colored pens and pencils to make their maps colorful and artistic. Those who always complained about having to write anything also complained about concept mapping, but when I asked the student focus group about the concept maps that we constructed for each module, they replied as follows:

- "It helps me to remember the differences between similar concepts."
- "They help me to study."
- "I can close my eyes and see the concept maps. This helps me on tests."
- "It's good to know why we are doing the things we do."

Students commented that constructing the smaller concept maps on their own was much harder, but some liked the activity because "it made me think hard."

Perhaps the greatest value in concept mapping as a teaching/learning activity was that it required me to review what students had already learned whenever we added new concepts to the map. I also found it to be a much more interactive form of direct instruction than simple lecture.

Because ninth graders enter our program with such varied science backgrounds, I found it essential to help them to develop a common and rich scientific vocabulary. With the modules providing readings for each investigation, I chose to highlight from those readings scientific terms that have basic Latin and Greek roots embedded in them. By focusing on the roots of scientific words, I could help students not only learn and remember the meaning of the words they were currently encountering, but also be able to predict the meaning of words they encountered later on. Thus, with each investigation, I led students through the dissection of a handful of terms. The students were tested periodically on their retention of and ability to apply the roots they learned. With time, the students demonstrated a rich vocabulary and the ability to recognize roots when they encountered new words.

I was quite pleased with student response to and achievement in vocabulary development during the use of these modules. My observation was that learning and recognizing Latin and Greek roots removes the need to memorize vocabulary words in science. Instead, students can see a root word, think about a word that has this root for which they already know the meaning, and then use their prior knowledge to understand the new term. On the prequestionnaire, students commented that "remembering the differences between similar words" and "remembering different terms and vocabulary" were difficult. After being exposed to Latin and Greek roots as a means of developing vocabulary, students responded on the postquestionnaire to the question, "Do you feel that breaking down vocabulary words into their Latin and Greek roots has helped you to learn and recall the meaning of these words and words similar to them?" as follows: 54 percent yes, 19 percent no, and 27 percent maybe.

4. Use of Module Notebooks to Manage Student Work

During my five years of teaching ninth graders, I have experimented with a variety of methods for managing student work. No single method seemed to meet the developmental and maturity levels of all 32 ninth graders in my room. I began my career collecting student work daily. But then I found that, in addition to being completely inundated by grading, students would turn in their work and forget about it. They would rarely reflect on it or keep it for later use. I gradually moved to asking students to maintain a class notebook. The first notebooks I experimented with were spiral bound. Students would write notes, labs, activities, and homework directly in this notebook. Any sheets that were passed out were folded and taped onto notebook paper. I would then collect these notebooks about every four weeks or so, just before the end of a grading period. But the notebooks fell apart, the handouts from me were not taped, and everything was out of order, not to mention that the wires of the spirals constantly intertwined with other notebooks, making them very difficult to separate. At the end of a semester, the notebooks were thick and cumbersome. Next I asked students to maintain hard-bound, composition-style notebooks. But again, papers were lost, history assignments found their way onto the pages of science, and grading the extremely out-of-order collection of scribble was nearly impossible.

When I implemented of these modules, I also changed the way I managed student work. The modules are small and soft-bound. To prevent wear and tear on the expensive packages, I hole-punched the modules so that students could secure them in three-ring binders. This led to me requiring students to have a science binder, with only science material kept in it. Thus the science binder holds the module, an assignment log, and notebook paper. Now students do everything on a separate sheet of notebook paper. They title the page, fill it up, and place it behind the assignment log in chronological order. When I pass out handouts, these, too, are hole-punched and inserted behind the other papers in the notebook.

Either in the middle or at the end of a module, depending on the unit's length, I ask students to remove all of their papers, place them in the order they were written on the assignment log, and staple them behind the assignment log. Then they turn in this packet of work for evaluation. For some modules I require that a cover for the stapled notebook be illustrated to demonstrate student learning. It sounds so simple, yet I cannot believe it has taken five years of teaching freshmen to arrive at this revelation. This system works! I actually receive the majority of the required work from most students. Lost papers are not as large a problem, and with daily stamping of homework, procrastination is not as rampant either. When students turn in their module notebooks, they are much more organized, of higher quality, and easier to grade.

Since each module starts fresh as a new notebook, this system also reduced the volume of work that students were maintaining daily. I reminded students that if they kept the already graded module notebooks, they could use them on the semester final. In addition, what I might like best about this method of managing student work is that after a discussion, readings, or working on the concept map, students can go back and change earlier answers. In fact, I give students an extra five-point homework stamp if they take the time to go back and edit their work.

I knew that I was finally pleased with how I was managing student work. But the most validating responses came from the students when I compared their prequestionnaire responses before piloting the modules to their postquestionnaire responses once they had kept a module notebook. I asked the students to comment on how student work was managed in class. The following statements are representative responses:

Prequestionnaire Responses:
- "I like not having to turn in work every day."
- "I don't like not knowing exactly what to keep and trying to keep everything."
- "Worksheets clutter up my notebook."
- "I lose my work when I don't turn it in right away."

- "I don't like how my papers fall out and the binding goes."
- "I have a hard time keeping an organized notebook."
- "The notebooks are too big and bulky."

Postquestionnaire Responses:

- "The notebook makes me keep my papers and look at them."
- "It helps me study for tests."
- "I like that I am learning how to stay organized."
- "I like that our work is corrected all at once."
- "It keeps me organized."
- "I like it because it doesn't take up much of my space."
- "I like that I only have to keep my papers for a little while."
- "The notebooks are an easy grade."
- "I like making covers for the notebook. It's fun."
- "It's good to get the chance to redo work and get it stamped again once you understand the material better."
- "It's easy for me to turn work in on time."

I also asked students if using an assignment log and smaller unit notebook would help them to keep a more organized notebook. They responded as follows:

Prequestionnaire Responses: *Postquestionnaire Responses:*
50 percent yes   74 percent yes
20 percent no   17 percent no
30 percent maybe   9 percent maybe

When asked if using an assignment log and smaller unit notebook would help them to turn in and complete their work, students responded:

Prequestionnaire Responses: *Postquestionnaire Responses:*
33 percent yes   63 percent yes
20 percent no   15 percent no
47 percent maybe   22 percent maybe

Conclusion

This is the first year that I have truly felt I am doing a good job teaching ninth graders. I'm happy with the academic approach, developmental level, scientific content, and experimental method of the curriculum, and I'm pleased with the level of organization, accountability, and communication within my class. Students have responded to the course with enthusiasm and effort. In addition, I feel I am providing a challenging yet accessible learning environment. I attribute these judgments to a good curriculum, successful management of 100-minute class periods, and development of clear and consistent classroom routines.

Before implementation of these instructional practices, students commented as follows:

- "I don't like that we can't bring a class book home."
- "It's bad that there aren't enough books for everyone."
- "It's too easy to fall behind in class."
- "It's hard for me to keep up on class work when I can't take anything home."
- "It's hard to get and do make-up work."
- "Doing labs that I don't understand frustrates me."
- "We don't get enough done in class."
- "It's hard to remember everything."
- "If you miss a day you're lost."

Now, after implementation of this project, the biggest complaints I hear are these: "We're too busy all the time," "How come we have to read and answer questions in science class?" and "We do too many labs." But even with these complaints, I know that student learning and achievement have improved. When asked on the prequestionnaire to rate how well they felt they understood the concepts and vocabulary presented in class, students responded: 2 percent not at all, 27 percent kind of, 58 percent fairly well, and 13 percent very well. After using the modules and implementing instructional practices to accommodate their successful use in the block schedule, the students responded to the same question on the postquestionnaire: 4 percent not at all, 16.5 percent kind of, 29 percent fairly well, and 50.5 percent very well.

Perhaps the most profound marker of change in student learning and achievement as a result of this project was the improvement in my students' notebook grades, which are a measure not only of learning but of work completion, as well. In the pilot group last spring, the average scores for the two classes on three notebooks were: 61 percent, 64.5 percent, and 65.8 percent (with an average of two zero grades per class). But notebook grades for these same students, for the two pilot modules, improved to an average of 72 percent and 74.6 percent (again with an average of two zero grades per class). I was amazed to see this improvement because the two module ones were the only ones that contained detailed homework. This year my students, who have used the modules and the classroom procedures discussed in this study since the first day of school, have achieved notebook scores of 81 percent, 79.33 percent, 78.32 percent, and 82.2 percent (for four modules, averaged total scores for all three classes, with an average of two zeros per class). I have reason to be confident in this new curriculum and my attempt to implement inquiry learning in the 100-minute block schedule. I hope with time, as I refine and focus my instructional practices and reflect on my relationship to my students' success, student learning and achievement in my classroom will continue to improve.

Appendix A

Integrated Physical Science Student Questionnaire I

1. Rate how well you feel you understand the concepts and vocabulary presented in class:

Not at All	Kind Of	Fairly Well	Very Well
(1)	(2)	(3)	(4)

2. With the exception of daily warm-ups, do you feel you know what to expect when you come to class?

Definitely No	Sometimes	Usually	Definitely Yes
(1)	(2)	(3)	(4)

3. If you had a small science workbook with science information, readings, and prewritten labs.

   a. Do you think your learning would improve?

   Yes   No   Maybe

   b. Would this help you to keep a more organized notebook?

   Yes   No   Maybe

   c. Would this help you keep up with daily work or make-up work when you were absent?

   Yes   No   Maybe

   d. Would this give you more resources for completing projects?

   Yes   No   Maybe

4. If you had regular assignments, so you always knew what to expect on "A" days, would this help you turn in and complete your work?

   Yes   No   Maybe

5. If you were able to read a lab a day before it was done in class, would this help you understand the lab and extract meaning from the activity?

   Yes   No   Maybe

6. What do you like and/or dislike about the way your notebook is currently used and managed in class?

7. What is your greatest difficulty in science class?

Appendix B

Integrated Physical Science Student Questionnaire II

1. Rate how well you feel you understood the concepts and vocabulary presented in the module, *Electricity and Magnetism*, compared to other units we have studied in class:

Not at All	Kind Of	Fairly Well	Very Well
(1)	(2)	(3)	(4)

2. Do you feel that the use of modules in science has created daily routines that allow you to plan for class and know what is expected of you:

Definitely No	Sometimes	Usually	Definitely Yes
(1)	(2)	(3)	(4)

3. Do you feel that the use of modules with short readings in science has:
    a. Helped your learning to improve?

    Yes   No   Maybe

    b. Helped you to keep up with daily work or make-up work when you were absent?

    Yes   No   Maybe

    c. Allowed you to better understand labs and extract meaning from activities?

    Yes   No   Maybe

4. Do you feel that the use of an assignment log and a smaller unit notebook has helped you to:
    a. Keep a more organized notebook?

    Yes   No   Maybe

    b. Turn in and complete your work?

    Yes   No   Maybe

5. Do you feel that breaking vocabulary words into the Latin and Greek roots has helped you to learn and recall the meaning of these words and words similar to them?

    Yes   No   Maybe

6. What do you like and/or dislike about the use of modules in science class?

PART 2

Teaching and Learning in the Block Period

3

Effective Sequencing of Varied Teaching/ Learning Activities in Block Periods

Allen Olson
Cedarcrest High School

According to Allen Olson, "it was clear from my own teaching experience that one of the most difficult aspects of teaching in block periods was planning the sequence of activities that would make the most effective use of available time." He knew from teaching experience and prior research that the variety of activities was a key to their effectiveness. But what created enough variety? In what sequence(s) should activities be organized?

Olson's study explores his own and his students' perceptions about the answers to these questions and provides several guidelines for instructional planning in block periods. He explains, "Different types of activities that are useful and engaging for most students can be incorporated into sequences that provide a balance of individual and group activities, active and passive activities, independent and interactive activities, silent and social activities. Weaving these different types of activities together breaks up the block period while maintaining a sense of order."

Introduction

Finding activities that can be used to break up the large block of time available in a 100-minute period is essential. Finding activities that can be woven into an efficient and effective sequence that enhances students' mastery of the course objectives is the challenge of teaching in block periods. After teaching introductory level, required science classes for three years in the 100-minute periods at Cedarcrest High School, I have collected quite a few different activities. This project presents some of these activities and student evaluations of them.

From my perspective, just as important as the activities is the methodology incorporated into this project. By using some of the principles and methods of personal construct psychology, I investigated what students perceived to be the important characteristics of a number of teaching/learning activities. The effort to investigate students' perceptions is an important part of the educational process that is too often neglected. It is in this sense that the methodology of this project may be just as important as the findings.

School Setting

Cedarcrest High School in Duvall, Washington, has been on an extended block period schedule since it opened in the fall of 1993. Duvall is a small town 30 miles east of Seattle, and the school includes small-town, rural, and rapidly growing suburban and exurban populations. The "Cedarcrest Plan" called for a three-period day. Each student is enrolled in three, 100-minute classes at a time. The school year is split into four nine-week terms, with each teacher having a 100-minute prep period for half of the year. Thus, each teacher still teaches the equivalent of five classes, the norm in a six-period day schedule. Most departments' courses are 18 weeks long.

Previous Research

In a previous action research study at Cedarcrest High School, Alexander, Lovre, Olson, and Smith came to several conclusions about the use of activities in block periods.

> The primary message of our research in terms of its application to the classroom is variety. The fact that our discovered themes of *variety*, *organization*, and *involvement* are rather obvious does not make them any less important. As teachers, this discovery will push us to be more self-conscious of our own use of variety in the classroom. It focuses our attention on the need to plan different activities and transitions between activities to maximize our effectiveness in 100 minutes. (Alexander, Lovre, Olson, and Smith, 1997, p. 106)

The previous Cedarcrest study involved surveys of the entire faculty, interviews of all administrators, and a random sample of the faculty and students. Because of its scope, it was not able to make specific suggestions about what activities can be used in block periods. Instead, it offered insights about the types of activities and the general strategies teachers should use when planning for block periods. The project mentioned several areas for further research, including questions concerning the most effective types and sequences of activities in block periods.

The Current Research Question

As I began my current study, I created a research question that I hoped would focus more narrowly on the same topics we had studied in the previous year. It was clear from my own teaching experience that one of the most difficult aspects of teaching in block periods was planning the sequence of activities that would make the most effective use of available time. The sequence in which variety was offered had not been investigated in the previous study. To make my research as valuable as possible to other teachers, I wanted to keep the characteristics that defined *sequence* as general as possible while using concrete examples of actual activities that seem to work in my own classroom. I therefore settled on the following research question:

> What types of activities can be used in a block period to provide enough variety to keep students engaged?

This question is intentionally vague and serves mainly as a reminder that variety is the key to successful teaching in block periods. The subquestions that must be answered to clarify this research question include:

1. What characteristics of activities are most important in planning the activities to be used in a block period?
2. What sequence of activities allows the block period to run efficiently?

The first subquestion was the major driving force in my research and is the basis for most of the data presented below. However, the second question is the most important because it provides the motivation for the first question.

My own experience of teaching in 100-minute periods suggests that the following general sequence works well:

1. Start with a medium to long individual activity.
2. In the middle of the period, provide one or two different activities that involve group work, or at least allow students to move around and change their focus of attention.
3. End the period with either a short or medium-length individual activity.

This sequence has some obvious variations and is general enough to be used in almost any course or classroom. This general format is what I attempt to use daily in my classroom. I find that when I am able to direct this sequence of activities for students, I generally have fewer discipline problems and more engagement than when I do not follow this sequence. Also note this sequence is compatible with the results of the research of Alexander, Lovre, Olson, and Smith, who reported the following:

> Students even had suggestions for the best way to organize activities. They liked to have a short review of material at the beginning of class with some time for questions to be answered. A quick lecture or instruc-

tions for a lab or activity should follow this. Then group work and individual practice time would take up the majority of the period. The period would end with a discussion and some instructions about how to prepare for the next day . . . Teachers mentioned a general goal of three different activities per class period, all focused on the same set of concepts but coming at them from different angles and utilizing different learning styles. As with the students, teachers mentioned review, introduction of new material, individual practice and group work, and a final check of understanding as a good pattern to follow. (Alexander, Lovre, Olson, and Smith, p. 104)

The review, present, practice, check, and preview sequence clearly follows the same general pattern as the sequence I have suggested; however, it does not outline specific activities to include. To achieve that level of focus requires some clarification and evaluation of the characteristics of individual activities. This, in turn, requires an answer to the first subquestion: What characteristics of activities are most important in planning the activities to be used in a block period?

Using a combination of my own experience and current knowledge concerning effective teaching practice, I identified the following to be the most important concerns of a teacher who is planning activities for use in a block period:

- course objectives
- student learning styles
- teaching styles
- time
- variety
- class size and composition

If these are the concerns that must be kept in mind when planning an activity, then they should be kept in mind while investigating and evaluating activities. They are, therefore, the concerns that underlie my research question and that determined what information would be included about the activities evaluated in this project.

However, the concerns listed above do not translate directly into characteristics. Concerns about student learning styles, teaching styles, and variety are the most important for determining what characteristics are important, and they are somewhat interdependent. What seems to be most important, and possibly the entire reason why variety is important, is that students have different learning styles that must be respected and different needs that must be met. My belief is that at the top of the list of needs and styles are the following:

- Students need movement.
- Teachers need whole-class instructional time.

- People need interaction.
- Individuals need to be responsible for their own learning.
- *The focus of attention needs to change so that the attention can remain focused.*

This list of needs and styles does lead finally to some characteristics of activities. What is important about a teaching/learning activity for its use in a block period sequence is the amount of movement allowed by the activity, the size of the group involved in the activity, the amount of interaction allowed by the activity, and the focus of attention of the activity.

My claim is simple. An effective sequence of activities for a block period involves some activities that do not allow movement balanced by activities that do. It has some activities that involve large-group direct instruction balanced by activities that involve small-group cooperative work or individual, self-sustained study. It has activities with limited interaction balanced by activities that allow more active interaction. Overall, it keeps students focused by changing their focus.

With these insights in mind, I returned to the original research question and attempted to find activities that could be used to keep students engaged throughout the block period.

The Data Collection Plan

To answer my research question, it seemed best to attempt to create a catalogue of classroom activities that described and were rated from the perspective of both the teacher and the student. Such a catalogue would allow teachers to select activities that fit into sequences that promote student engagement, help students master course content, minimize disruptions and discipline problems, and provide the variety that is necessary in block periods. I have created a format for such a catalogue, which allows other teachers to add their own activities to the listing and to use the methods I have used to reflect on their own teaching by collecting teacher and student evaluations of classroom activities.

The information that the catalogue should provide about each activity can be derived from the answer to subquestion 1 above. Most of this information can be provided directly by the teacher. However, it is important to include students' perceptions of the characteristics of the activities, which can be compared to the perceptions of the teacher.

Collecting students' perceptions about classroom activities can be accomplished in several ways. Typical methods are interviews and surveys; however, it is often difficult to use these methods to get simple data about student perceptions without providing limiting and possibly leading questions. A method used in psychology to investigate the perceptions of other people involves eliciting characteristics from an interviewee and then using those characteristics to survey the interviewee's perceptions of the subjects being investigated. This method is based on the personal construct psychology of George Kelly (1955). The method can be time-consuming if done as precisely as Kelly and others propose (see Fransella and Bannister, 1977, for a thorough explanation of the technique), but it provides a wealth of data that can be analyzed subjectively and objectively and are relatively free of interviewer bias if done properly.

The methodology used by personal construct psychologists to investigate an individual's perceptions about a certain subject area requires that the individual be interviewed and asked methodically to compare and contrast the objects, ideas, or examples of the subject area. The compare-and-contrast exercise results in a list of characteristics that can be used by the interviewee to rate those same objects, ideas, or examples. These ratings can be analyzed objectively to evaluate the individual's perceptions about the degree of similarity among the characteristics that were used to make the ratings. The objects, ideas, or examples that were rated can also be evaluated for similarity according to the individual's perceptions. These objective correlations can be very revealing to both the researcher and the individual.

For this research project, I decided to cut a few corners while still subscribing to the general methodology of personal construct psychology. Instead of interviewing individuals, I used classroom discussions to elicit characteristics about the classroom activities I had used. These characteristics were then compiled into a rating sheet, which students used to rate activities they liked and disliked. These rating sheets were analyzed briefly to see if any conclusions could readily be drawn about the characteristics the students had identified.

Specifically, the student evaluation portion of my research was conducted as follows:

1. The students from each class period brainstormed a list of the activities used in the class.
2. Students were asked to make a list of the three activities they liked the most and thought were the most useful, and another list of the three activities they liked the least or thought were the least useful.
3. Students were asked to explain why certain activities were "good" and others "bad" by looking for similarities in the three activities they liked and contrasting those activities with the ones they disliked.
4. The explanations from step 3 were used to create a list of characteristics of activities.
5. For each characteristic on the list from step 4, students were asked, "What is the opposite of that?" It was emphasized that a new term was needed to describe the contrasting idea. For example, "not competitive" is not acceptable as the opposite of "competitive." (This is a very important distinction in personal construct psychology.)
6. The resulting list of characteristics and their opposites was made into an evaluation sheet without numbers so that there would be no assumption that any

characteristic was intrinsically "better" or "worse" than its opposite (see appendix A).

7. Students were asked to evaluate the different activities used in the class (the activities brainstormed in step 1). It was emphasized that each characteristic was not necessarily better or worse than its opposite. Students were instructed to indicate whether or not they liked the activity they were evaluating, and attempts were made to ensure that each of the activities that were the focus of this study was evaluated by students who liked the activity and students who disliked the activity.

8. The evaluation sheets were collected and converted into numerical ratings that could be analyzed objectively.

This methodology was used to elicit general student perceptions of classroom activities. More precise data could be collected by conducting interviews that took individual students through this process. This would give insight into the particular preferences and learning styles of those students and provide information about how certain activities fit those individual learning styles. A general catalogue of activities would be enhanced by such individual data, but the wider perceptions of groups of students are the first pieces of information I chose to collect.

Catalogue of Activities

The following list of activities used in my science classroom resulted from three brainstorming sessions with my students. Only the first nine of these were investigated fully, and these are included in the catalogue of activities below.

• Labs the students do
• Labs the teacher does for the whole class
• Lectures with demonstrations
• Lectures without demonstrations
• Pop-up review
• Guesser game
• Bucket questions
• Preparing and giving presentations
• Listening to others' presentations
• Discussion
• Quizzes and tests
• Reading, outlining, and answering text questions
• Video
• Group grading of other period's tests
• Free work time

Labs the Students Do

The labs that students do are generally considered to be the most popular part of my class and most science classes. They are fairly simple, never taking more than half an hour to conduct. However, the time spent preparing to conduct the experiment and discussing the results often makes the entire activity one of the longest I use. The prepare-predict-conduct-summarize format for labs follows the sequence students and teachers suggested in the previous Cedarcrest study. In other words, the labs that students do can be broken down into smaller activities that follow the sequence of activities suggested above.

- *objectives:* procedural skills, reinforces content
- *learning styles:* kinesthetic, hands-on, visual
- *student engagement and excitement:* generally high
- *focus of attention:* lab apparatus, results
- *group size:* individual prelab preparation, small-group experimenting, large-group postlab discussion
- *activity length:* flexible length but generally long
- *preparation time:* content-dependent but generally demanding
- *discipline issues:* lack of cooperation, group-group interaction, lack of participation, too much socializing

Student Evaluation

Students were generally in agreement that labs give hands-on experience, allow socializing, allow movement, help understanding, involve group interdependence, and are active, attention-getting, interactive, cooperative, and useful.

There was more reserved agreement that labs help students explain; help their memory through trial and error, and are simple, exciting, and engaging.

The most disagreement was about whether the activity could hold students' interest for a long time and whether it reveals what the student knows.

Labs the Teacher Does for the Whole Class

Sometimes a lab is too complicated, too dangerous, or requires too many materials for the students to do it. I do these labs as a demonstration in front of the whole class, but we generally have the traditional prelab preparation and postlab discussion, so the activity is not the same as a lecture with a demonstration.

- *objectives:* reinforces content
- *learning styles:* visual, auditory
- *student engagement and excitement:* generally high
- *focus of attention:* teacher, lab apparatus, results

- *group size:* individual prelab preparation, large-group demonstration and discussion
- *activity length:* flexible length, generally shorter than a student lab
- *preparation time:* content-dependent, generally demanding but less demanding than a student lab
- *discipline issues:* general large-group distractions—lack of attention, talking

Student Evaluation

This was perceived as an activity in which students listen and watch and cannot talk, and that helps them explain and understand; gives them the right answers; holds their interest; and is useful, attention-getting, and exciting.

There was more reserved agreement that teacher-conducted labs were complex.

The most disagreement was about whether the activity was passive or active, and how the activity affected their grade.

Lectures with Demonstrations

Although lectures take longer to prepare if a demonstration is involved, the demonstration always serves as an attention-getting device that helps keep the students focused. For that reason, I consider lectures with and without demonstrations to be different activities.

- *objectives:* present or reinforce content
- *learning styles:* visual, auditory
- *student engagement and excitement:* medium
- *focus of attention:* teacher and demonstration apparatus
- *group size:* large group
- *activity length:* flexible length, but generally 15–30 minutes
- *preparation time:* demonstration preparation can be demanding; preparation of lecture notes is a demanding, one-time investment
- *discipline issues:* general large-group distractions—lack of attention, talking

Student Evaluation

There was agreement that this is an activity in which students listen and watch and cannot talk or move around. It also helps them explain and understand; gives them the right answers; affects future grades; and is individual, passive, and useful.

The activity was seen as neither attention-getting nor dull, neither exciting nor boring, and it was rated right in the middle between "holds my interest for a long time" and "only good for a short time."

The greatest disagreement concerned whether the activity shows what students know or whether it doesn't matter what students know.

Lectures without Demonstrations

- *objectives:* present or reinforce content
- *learning styles:* visual, auditory
- *student engagement and excitement:* low to medium
- *focus of attention:* teacher
- *group size:* large group
- *activity length:* flexible length, but generally 10 to 20 minutes
- *preparation time:* one-time investment in creation of good notes is demanding but necessary
- *discipline issues:* general large-group distractions—lack of attention, talking

Student Evaluation

The student evaluations of lectures were very uniform. There was agreement that this is an activity in which students listen and watch and cannot talk or move around. It helps them explain and tells them what; gives them the right answers; helps their memory through repetition; affects future grades; and is simple, passive, dull, solitary, independent, boring, long, but useful.

The greatest disagreement concerned whether the activity was individual or group dependent.

Pop-up Review

In this activity, students move from seat to seat in the room. At each seat there is a question for them to answer on their own sheet of paper. Each seat also has the answer to the previous question, so students know immediately if their answer is right. The students move from seat to seat on a signal that occurs at regular intervals (usually 30 to 60 seconds).

- *objectives:* reinforce content, review for tests
- *learning styles:* linguistic, recall
- *student engagement and excitement:* medium
- *focus of attention:* individual questions
- *group size:* everyone works individually
- *activity length:* depends on number of students in class and time allowed per question; usually 15–30 minutes
- *preparation time:* one set of questions must be written; questions must be of similar difficulty so that students can complete each in the same amount of time
- *discipline issues:* students must remain silent; otherwise, activity is entirely self-maintaining

Student Evaluation

Some students liked this activity; others disliked it strongly. However, both types of student agreed that the pop-up review is an activity in which students cannot talk. It tells them what, gives them the right answers, affects future grades, and is individual and independent.

Students who liked the activity also found it to be useful. However, students who did not like it found it unnecessary, simple, long, boring, dull, passive, and felt that it did not allow them to move around. These opinions were not shared by students who liked the activity.

Guesser Game

In this activity, students compete in teams in a game similar to *Password* or *$500,000 Pyramid*. A set of terms are written on cards, and one member of the team is seated facing the rest of the team so that he or she cannot see the card. The other team members take turns giving the "guesser" hints to get the "guesser" to say the term on the card. The card is flipped to the next card when the guesser guesses or passes. Points are awarded for good clues and for each term the guesser correctly guesses. The guesser can make only one guess for each term, but the other team members can give any number of clues. The team has a certain amount of time in each round (usually a minute or two), and teams try to get as many points as possible in each round.

- *objectives:* reinforce vocabulary, review for tests
- *learning styles:* linguistic, recall
- *student engagement and excitement:* high
- *focus of attention:* competitors and vocabulary used in the game
- *group size:* teams of four to eight students compete against each other
- *activity length:* 10–30 minutes
- *preparation time:* one set of terms must be written on cards
- *discipline issues:* students must remain silent when their team is not competing; students must be quieted down after transition from one team to the next

Student Evaluation

Most students strongly liked this activity; a few others disliked it. All agreed that the guesser game shows what you know, is group dependent, is active, and helps memory through repetition.

Students who disliked the activity said that it required them to be still and ranked the activity as more competitive than those who liked the activity.

Students who liked the activity found it more exciting, engaging, simple, and useful than students who did not like it.

Bucket Questions

In this activity, a series of questions are written on small pieces of paper that are wadded up and put in a bucket. Each student pulls a question out of the bucket as it is passed around the room. The students have a short time to make sure they can explain the answer to that question to the rest of the class, then each student is called on in random order. The students are expected to summarize the answer the previous student gave and then give their own question and answer to the class. Although this activity was successful, I will change it in the future to make small groups answer a related set of questions so the activity goes faster.

- *objectives:* reinforce content, review for tests, communication skills, summarizing, paraphrasing, and explaining skills
- *learning styles:* verbal, recall
- *student engagement and excitement:* low
- *focus of attention:* other individual students in the class
- *group size:* individual responsibility in whole class exercise
- *activity length:* about a minute per student plus 10 minutes at the beginning for students to prepare their answers
- *preparation time:* at least one question per student must be written on pieces of paper
- *discipline issues:* students must remain silent and pay attention while other students give their answers (this is difficult to maintain for the length of time required to get to every student)

Student Evaluation

This activity was disliked by most students and liked by only a few. All agreed that the activity was individual, but that is about all they agreed on. Even among students who disliked the activity, there was very little agreement on whether the activity was unnecessary or useful, active or passive, complex or simple, and repetitious or trial and error. They did agree that the activity was long, boring, dull, solitary, only good for a short time, and shows what you know. The students who liked the activity found it more engaging and useful and said that it helped them explain.

Preparing and Giving Presentations

For the last two weeks of class, students work together in groups on presentations they will use to teach a topic to the class. They prepare visual aids, worksheets, a quiz, and a lab or demonstration if appropriate. In the future, I will not have the whole class doing this at the same time because it is too demanding on my time to be on call for all the groups at the same time. I probably will spread the presentations out over the entire course.

- *objectives:* research skills, communication skills, mastery of a topic, cooperative work, block project planning skills, organization skills
- *learning styles:* visual, kinesthetic, verbal, and others
- *student engagement and excitement:* medium

- *focus of attention:* the research topic
- *group size:* groups of two to four people
- *activity length:* 20–40 minutes of in-class work time given daily for one or two weeks
- *preparation time:* clear grading criteria must be developed; helping to find and limit sources can be demanding
- *discipline issues:* keeping students on task and on schedule; very difficult to manage all groups at the same time

Student Evaluation

This activity was liked by all the students who chose to evaluate it. They found it gave them hands-on experience; helped them explain; had an immediate effect on their grade; held their interest; and was cooperative, useful, attention-getting, interactive, simple, and long.

The most disagreement on the evaluations was evident in trying to classify the activity as active or passive.

Listening to Others' Presentations

The natural consequence of preparing presentations is that they must be presented. However, having all the presentations at once at the end of the course violates the objective of variety because most of the class must remain seated and attentive throughout the presentations. Having different topics presented provides variety, but does not provide the necessary variety in types of activities. Therefore, having the presentations spread out throughout the course is better than having them all presented at the same time.

- *objectives:* model communication and presentation skills for the audience; provide audience with brief introduction to many topics
- *learning styles:* verbal; visual
- *student engagement and excitement:* low
- *focus of attention:* other groups of students
- *group size:* small groups presenting to whole class
- *activity length:* each presentation can last 10–30 minutes depending on directions from teacher and planning of students
- *preparation time:* teacher must have good grading criteria prepared
- *discipline issues:* students must remain silent while group is presenting

Student Evaluation

Students who liked this activity and those who did not agreed that the activity was one in which you sit and listen, cannot talk, and must remain still. They also agreed that it did not matter what you knew, that the activity was only good for a short time, and that it was cooperative and group dependent.

Students who liked the activity said that it helped them understand and that it affected future grades. Even though they did not find the activity as boring, dull, unnecessary, and solitary as those who disliked the activity, those who liked it still ranked it more on that side than on the exciting, engaging, and useful side.

Findings and Analysis

In addition to the catalogue of activities, my research produced some information about student attitudes toward classroom activities. Some of this information is evident in the above summaries of student evaluations. Other information comes from looking at all of the evaluations as a whole and at different subsets of the evaluations, such as the evaluations from students who liked the activity they were evaluating and those who did not. Without providing all the data that were used in the analysis, it is possible to state some not necessarily surprising findings that help to confirm some notions about and frustrations of teaching.

First of all, it is clear from the student evaluations that no real pattern can be used to predict whether students will like or dislike an activity. Obviously, students do not usually like activities that are dull and boring; but what some students find dull and boring, others find attention-getting, interesting, and engaging. Note also that students who found an activity to be dull and boring sometimes liked it anyway and found it to be useful. The strongest negative evaluations by students focused on long, boring, in-class activities that do not allow for movement or socializing and hold one's interest only for a short time. The biggest differences in evaluations of "liked" and "not liked" activities were in interest, excitement, and engagement.

None of this is surprising, or that helpful, either. The usual dilemma facing teachers is how to develop and use activities that are exciting and engaging and still accomplish the course objectives. It would be helpful to know what makes an activity "exciting" or "engaging," but this depends greatly on the individual student. Thus, in looking at the general evaluations of many students, no characteristics seem to be indicative of "exciting" or "engaging." This can be analyzed objectively by looking at the correlations among the different characteristics that students used to evaluate activities. By defining the "distance" between two characteristics as the absolute value of the difference between their ratings on any individual activity, one can find a normalized, average correlation coefficient between two characteristics. When this was done with all the evaluations of activities that were completed by students, the only significant correlations were:

- D indicates the correlation was only significant among evaluations from students who disliked the activity they were evaluating.
- L indicates the correlation was only significant among evaluations from students who liked the activity they were evaluating.
- Correlations with no superscript were significant among evaluations by both sets of students.

"boring"	is highly correlated with	"dull / bland"[D] "I have to be still"[D] "I zone out / lose interest"[D] "I sit and listen / watch"[D]
"dull / bland"	is highly correlated with	"I sit and listen / watch" "I have to be still" "independent" "solitary" "I zone out / lose interest" "passive listening / writing"[L] "only good for a short time"[D] "I can't talk"[D] "helps memory by giving right answers"[D]
"I zone out / lose interest"	is highly correlated with	"unnecessary"[L] "only good for a short time"[D] "I can't talk"[D] "I sit and listen"[D] "I have to be still"[D] "solitary"[D]
"I can't talk"	is highly correlated with	"I have to be still" "only good for a short time"[D]
"I sit and listen/ watch"	is highly correlated with	"I can't talk" "I have to be still" "helps memory by repetition"[L] "passive"[L] "solitary"[D]
"solitary"	is highly correlated with	"passive" "independent" "I can't talk"[L] "individual"[D]
"passive"	is highly correlated with	"independent"[L] "I can't talk"[L]
"exciting"	is highly correlated with	"holds my interest for a long time" "short"

"competitive"   is highly correlated with   "shows what I know"[D]

"tells me *what*"   is highly correlated with   "helps memory by repetition"[L]

"complex"   is highly correlated with   "immediately affects grade"[D]

Most of these correlations are not surprising, although the fact that they are evident in the data does support the data's validity. That is, one hopes that students' use of "solitary" and "independent" is similar for each activity that they evaluated. However, there are pieces of the data that undermine their own validity. For instance, "exciting" is not highly correlated with "attention-getting" as one might expect it to be.

What is interesting is that the above correlations are the most significant ones in the evaluations. "Exciting" is not correlated with "competitive." "Boring" is not highly correlated with "I can't talk." This means that competitive activities are not always exciting, and at least some students find some activities in which they cannot talk to be exciting. Again, there is no surprise here. Instead, it provides satisfying justification for the findings of the previous research project at Cedarcrest and the assumptions of this research project: *students differ, so variety is the key.* As long as different types of activities are used, all students will be able to find something exciting and engaging during the class period. However, if only one or two types of activities are used, it will be more difficult to meet the need and desires of all students.

There are other interesting findings in the above correlations, especially in the differences of opinion between students who liked and disliked the activities they were evaluating (bear in mind that the same activities were being evaluated). First, nothing was correlated with "boring" for students who liked the activity they were evaluating, and the only thing that was correlated with "I zone out / lose interest" for these students was "unnecessary." This should reinforce the earlier Cedarcrest study and other research that shows that it is important to tell students why they are doing what they are doing. When students understand how an activity is useful, they are more likely to accept it and allow themselves to be engaged by it.

On the other hand, it is clear from the correlations that activities in which students work independently, where they have to be still and cannot talk, and where they just sit and listen are more likely to be viewed as dull, bland, and boring and are less likely to keep students engaged. This, again, is not surprising; it is simply a reminder of the difficulties involved with large-group, direct instruction.

However, the student evaluations do indicate that some activities in which students are silent are viewed as useful. The pop-up review activity is a prime example of an activity that was accepted by students, though in some cases grudgingly, because it was clearly useful. It was still ranked as boring by students who did not like it, and it fell in the middle between boring and exciting for students who liked it. But it was rated as very useful by all but a few of the students who evaluated it. Lectures were accepted and given high marks for usefulness, and even engagement when demonstrations were involved.

All of this is good news for teachers who are planning activities for block periods. Different types of activities that are useful and engaging for most students can be incorporated into sequences that provide a balance of individual and group activities, active and passive activities, independent and interactive activities, silent and social activities. Weaving these different types of activities together breaks up the block period while maintaining a sense of order. Students remain engaged because the focus of attention changes. This is the goal of teaching in block periods. The activities investigated in this project form a sufficient, if incomplete, set of activities to accomplish that goal.

Conclusions and Future Research

To teach effectively in block periods, a balance of different types of activities must be provided so that students can remain engaged. To accomplish this, a teacher must have a repertoire of many different activities, some of which should be similar in content and objective and different in style. Other activities can be designed for special purposes. With this collection of types of activities, the teacher can pull together three or four activities to use in each block period.

For example, on some days, the order of activities and time constraints may allow for a student lab. On other days, it may be best to have the teacher conduct the lab as a demonstration. Many of the same objectives can be met by these two activities, but one is a silent, whole-class activity, and the other is a small-group, socially interactive activity.

As another example, the pop-up review is a wonderful activity from the perspective of the teacher because it is self-maintaining, independent, and silent. The activity is successful because students do not have to remain completely still, they know immediately whether they are right, and they see that the activity helps their test grades. However, running this activity for the entire period would not be successful. It works best as a calming break between more interactive activities or as a settling way to begin or end the period.

Overall, the findings of this project suggest the following:

- It is possible to collect a wide range of activities that meet instructional objectives in different ways.
- It is important to take the time to explain to students what an activity is intended to accomplish so they can see its usefulness.
- No activity can do everything for everyone, but most activities do something good for someone.

- By paying attention to characteristics of activities such as movement, interaction, and group size, teachers can create sequences of activities that provide the proper balance and variety for maintaining the necessary level of student engagement and excitement in block periods while maintaining a manageable classroom atmosphere.

This research can be helpful to other teachers as the beginning of a catalogue of activities that can be used effectively in block periods. However, the most enlightening part of this project may be the methodology. The process of eliciting characteristics and their opposites from students, and then using those characteristics to investigate their knowledge and opinions is not used in education. The fact that this process is used in psychology to investigate the conceptual structures of individuals should be taken as a hint by educators. The methodology can be used for more than evaluation of classroom activities. It can provide insight into learning styles of students and even evaluate the level of understanding an individual has about a certain subject area. These applications of personal construct psychology deserve much more attention in education.

Two other areas of research that are suggested by this project involve creating sets and sequences of activities that work well together and taking an even narrower focus on individual activities to find what learning and teaching styles they consistently enhance. The first area would provide useful information for planning in block periods. The second would make it possible to create more tailored curriculum for special needs or for any other students. Again, it seems that the methodology of personal construct psychology is perfectly suited to such research.

Finally, the value of action research itself is again supported by this project. Being reflective about one's own teaching and attempting to find ways to generalize one's own methods for use by other teachers helps focus one's energies on improving education. As students well know, it is very easy to "zone out/lose interest" if you are not "engaged/involved."

Appendix A

Student Evaluation Sheet

Activity _____ Name _____

← ——— Place an X along the scale to "rate" the activity. ———→

| I sit and listen / watch | I___I___I___I__ | I get hands-on experience |

| I can't talk | I___I___I___I__ | I can socialize |

| I have to be still | I___I___I___I__ | I can move around |

| helps me explain | I___I___I___I__ | just helps me memorize |

| tells me *what* | I___I___I___I__ | helps me understand *how* |

| competitive | I___I___I___I__ | cooperative |

| group dependence | I___I___I___I__ | individual |

| immediately affects grade | I___I___I___I__ | affects future grades |

| shows what I know | I___I___I___I__ | doesn't matter what I know |

holds my interest for a long time	|___|___|___|__	only good for a short time

unnecessary	|___|___|___|__	useful

passive writing/listening	|___|___|___|__	active involvement

always in class	|___|___|___|__	sometimes outside of class

dull / bland	|___|___|___|__	attention-getting

solitary	|___|___|___|__	interactive

independent	|___|___|___|__	get help from the group

helps memory by repetition	|___|___|___|__	helps memory through experience

exciting	|___|___|___|__	boring

helps memory by giving right answers	|___|___|___|__	helps memory through trial and error

complex / complicated	|___|___|___|__	simple / understandable

short |___|___|___|__   long
            __|___|
      | | | |
          | |

I zone out / lose interest |___|___|___|__   I am engaged / involved
            __|___|
      | | | |
          | |

References

Alexander, F., Lovre, M., Olson, A., & Smith, A. (1997). Cedarcrest High School: The effectiveness of learning activities and the use of time in the block period. In D. Marshak. *Action research on block scheduling* (pp. 88–115). Larchmont, NY: Eye on Education.

Fransella, F. and Bannister, D. (1977). *A manual for repertory grid technique.* London: Academic Press.

Kelly, G. (1955). *The psychology of personal constructs.* New York: W. W. Norton & Company.

4

Participation and Problem Solving: Using the Block Period to Raise the Quality of Student Participation

David Sherman
Shorewood High School

David Sherman wanted to use action research to improve the effectiveness of a United Nations conference simulation in his tenth grade World Studies classes. He also wanted to integrate regular Internet use by his students within the context of this course.

Sherman set up a Web site that specified this assignment, the "United Nations Conference on Middle East Peace and Development," and engaged his students in conducting all of their preparatory research for the simulation on the Internet. Students learned to find relevant Web sites and to evaluate the quality of materials on a site in terms of authorship, searchability, timeliness, and quality of information. Sherman also explored the use of performance rubrics as a way to encourage his students to become more active and vocal in the simulation itself and to use various assignment structures for motivating his students to explore and apply problem-solving skills and for encouraging them to engage in effective collaboration before and during the simulation.

Throughout his research Sherman considered how each element of this unit was enhanced by the availability of 100-minute block periods.

Introduction and Research Questions

I might as well be honest—I like the block period. I would never go back to teaching a hectic six-period day. I thought I might be unable to engage in unbiased research about block schedules, but I am also keenly aware of the need to set my emotional preferences aside and examine carefully the effects of the block period on student learning. With this in mind, I set out to develop a research question that would require a more objective analysis of my preference and help me to improve my instructional practices within the block period.

I decided that I wanted to focus on the effects of the block period on a specific instructional activity in my discipline, social studies. So I chose to analyze the impact of the block period on a complex learning activity that instructed and assessed students in a variety of skills: technology, information literacy, and speech. In my tenth grade World Studies course we ended the school year with a simulation dealing with the modern Middle East (see appendix A). This simulation has a separate research component in which students gather information about a nation to which they have been assigned, analyze several regional conflicts related to peace and economic development, and develop proposals to resolve those conflicts. Students are provided with a description of seven agenda issues that will be addressed by the representatives at the simulated United Nations conference (see appendix B).

Last year our library media center was closed for remodeling. As a result I had to modify the research so that all information gathering was conducted over the Internet, and students were required to submit evaluations of some of the Web sites they used (see appendix C). To accomplish this task, students worked in pairs, and at least one in each pair had Internet access at home. Block periods enable students to work collegially and provide opportunity for a realistic debate environment. I wanted to explore how the activity could be adapted further to take advantage of the block period setting.

In the past I had made several observations about the nature of student performance on various aspects of the simulation. Students collaborating on research presented the same written work, but often did not participate equally during the simulation's oral debate and discussion. Although students succeeded in representing their nations realistically and argued effectively, the data collected during the research phase did not appear to stimulate students to begin the conference with solutions to problems. Additionally, the conference phase was evaluated less formally and was always rushed, thereby encouraging students to devalue the experience. Although students had reported in class evaluations that they thought the project was fun and engaging, I believed it had potential to be an even more dynamic and valuable educational experience.

In response to these conclusions, I posed the following research question:

> How can the Middle East Simulation activities be improved within the block period to achieve greater oral participation and better problem solving in the United Nations Conference phase of the activity?

This broad question inevitably led to some important and equally meaningful subquestions:

- What are students' experiences of collaboration during the research phase?
- How can the research phase be restructured to promote greater oral participation during the United Nations Conference phase?

- How can the research phase be restructured to promote better problem solving during the United Nations Conference phase?
- What kinds of rubrics can be employed to clarify expectations for students?
- How can the United Nations Conference phase be restructured to encourage greater oral participation by all students?

Research Methodology

I taught three tenth grade World Studies classes at Shorewood High School (described in chapter 1), and I planned to conduct this action research in all three. Two were heterogeneous classes, and one was an honors class.

Initially I planned on conducting preproject and postproject teacher focus groups with my colleagues who also teach tenth grade World Studies. I was curious about their experiences with their students' collaboration and their ideas about how to restructure the activities in this simulation. Unfortunately, the time constraints that inevitably create significant stress in May and June prevented our four-person team from meeting together formally. Instead, I had to rely on informal chats at lunch and after school. Though I did not consider this to be formal data collection, my colleagues' comments did provide a barometer to gauge how the activities were perceived by their students. I also solicited input from the team on the evaluation tools (see appendixes F, G, and H). Although we were unable to evaluate their effectiveness collaboratively after the simulation ended, each teacher used the same rubrics in his or her evaluation scheme, thereby assuring all tenth graders of significant consistency in relation to the expectations of this project.

Another form of teacher data was the notes I kept as we worked our way through the project. This journal became the basis for many of the findings that follow, specifically the answers to the subquestions that I posed initially. The notes also provided me with built-in reflection time that caused me to focus on my instructional practices while the project and this research were underway. As a result, I was able to implement minor changes as necessary.

Data from students were elicited from written feedback solicited at intervals for extra credit points throughout the simulation. Though this practice created a bias, my intention was to induce those students who were more able to reflect on their learning to articulate their experiences. In my judgment the insights of more grade-conscious students were more likely to tell me how to refine implementation of the activities. Moreover, with fewer student responses to review, it was easier to separate the wheat from the chaff. Nevertheless, I also recruited students from all ability levels to provide feedback throughout the project. At the beginning of the simulation, I gave each student a set of journal prompts that encouraged brief but focused responses (see appendix D).

Parent input was solicited using a survey that was provided to each student. Before the simulation began, I sent a letter home informing parents about the project and warning them that a questionnaire would follow in a few weeks. Since parents were in a better position than I was to assess the way students spent time researching, I hoped that the parent questionnaire would provide data that otherwise would not be available to me (see appendix E). Of the 85 questionnaires distributed to parents or guardians, 53 were returned. Considering these were due the day of final exams, I was content with the 63 percent return rate.

Findings

Teacher Data

My own journal entries and notes recorded the changes in instruction that I implemented throughout the project. Some of these reflections were created after discussions with colleagues; others were in response to specific instructional activities conducted as we worked through the project. Along with student journal responses, these reflections enabled me to evaluate the project while it was underway and address the initial questions posed for this research.

How can the research phase be restructured to promote greater oral participation during the United Nations Conference *phase?*

Before the project began, the team of four World Studies teachers met to review the instructional materials, the scope of the unit, and the sequence of activities. Two of us had previously had success with the simulation, so there was consensus that we would use this activity. When I raised the question of how to use our time more efficiently and improve the quality of student participation at the conference, the answers became apparent.

We decided to revise the unit with a focus on performance-based assessment. First, we would present the instructions for the simulation (see appendix A) and assign students to their nations during the first few days of the unit so they could begin to identify with the agenda issues (appendix B) from their country's perspective. Next, we reviewed the reading packet we use with students and resequenced the material to match the seven issues that would be debated at the conference. Third, we deleted topics that were not directly related to the conference issues to avoid confusing the students. We also labeled the readings in the packet with a Roman numeral for each issue to make the connections to the agenda issues explicit. Fourth, we agreed to discuss each conference agenda issue at the same time that we covered the related reading or video material. We also hoped to raise student interest throughout this period of teacher-centered instruction by emphasizing those nations mentioned specifically in these materials. Finally, we reordered the issues to place the most emotionally engaging topics first. Since the Arab-Israeli conflict includes political, social, and economic complexities, it was our first choice. To students used to seeing the world in black and white terms, this topic initially seemed straightforward. But as we moved through the topic they soon realized it was not so simple. When we explored through the next issues dealing with religious interpretation, water disputes, and economic development, students were better prepared to cope with the complex perspectives of their assigned nation.

How can the research phase be restructured to promote better problem solving during the United Nations Conference phase?

A single change made a huge difference: assigning the simulation roles and introducing the instructions at the beginning of the unit. We provided students with two to three weeks more time to research than we had in the past. In my classes, students had a full month from the introduction of the simulation to the first day their written material was due. This extended time line gave students more flexibility to schedule their research work with their partner and conduct this work. They could also spread out their research so that they narrowed their searches to the one or two agenda issues we covered in class each week. Unfortunately, we did not require students to demonstrate the fruits of their labors with staggered due dates. My colleagues and I chose, instead, to have all the student materials due on one or two dates as the conference began.

This decision was not an oversight. I chose to avoid student and parent complaints about too much work by emphasizing the homework that students were assigned in their reading packet. No matter what kind of periods one teaches in, there are still limits to how much outside work a student can be expected to present in class. In fact, the major limitation of our block period, seeing students only three times a week, may have limited my ability to track student work on the Internet as we worked through the topics in class.

One major change, however, was the use of the 100-minute period to teach some of the specific computer skills related to this project. Before going to the computer lab with students, I used a video projector and computer to walk students through the Middle East Simulation web page. By using this visual in conjunction with the text in the reading packet, I hoped to steer them away from reliance on the paper text. I also wanted to model for students how to use the Web site. For example, when it came time to describe the type of resources that students were required to locate and save to a disk, I was able to click on each resource type to highlight a list of sites. Then I went to a few of those sites and demonstrated what was available. In each class, I used the simulation's web page to show students who were not familiar with the Internet how easily they could navigate and locate sources, as long as they knew they could return to our web page to reorient themselves. The goal was to provide a safe haven in cyberspace from which students could explore comfortably.

Instead of printing information directly from the Internet, our library staff tries to save printer resources by having students save data in a text-only format and then print that text on a dot-matrix printer. Students saving their information to a disk so that I could verify their research was a technical skill for which I would hold students accountable. Another skill that I demonstrated, therefore, was saving information in a text-only format from one of our listed sites.

During the same class period, I demonstrated the Web site evaluation rubric that students would use (appendix C). I began with the simulation instructions that explain the requirement for Web site evaluations. Then I showed students that the evaluation form and criteria were also linked from our Web site. Finally, I went back to one of the resources I had located during the demonstration and asked students to help me evaluate the site. They used their copy of the criteria in their course reader, looked at the image of the Web site on the large screen, and walked through the evaluation process together as a group.

This entire demonstration lasted about 45 minutes, the time evenly divided among reviewing the project instructions, locating some sample resources, and using the Web site evaluation rubric. The block period provided an excellent opportunity to balance regular class work with this demonstration. Moreover, the time invested in this teacher-centered activity made the following student-centered activity much more effective.

We spent the whole next class session in the computer lab. I had already demonstrated the work they would do, so all that was left was to be explicit about how they should use their time in the lab. Our computer lab's Internet access is limited. There are 13 machines that have fast Internet connections, so after giving students directions, I sent three of the most reliable student groups off to the library to work. All students were expected to complete the following:

1. Navigate around the Middle East Simulation web page and reread the instructions.
2. Locate one of the general United States government sites for their country and practice saving that information to a disk.
3. Search around the list of resources for some potentially biased information and complete one Web site evaluation form for each teammate.

While students who had little or no experience on the Internet struggled to get started, every student in each class were able to accomplish these tasks within a single block period.

This was one of the clearest examples of how the longer block period outperforms a short period. Students were able to focus on their work uninterrupted, which encouraged them to use their time more effectively. I observed students reading their packets and trying to understand the conference agenda issues while searching for specific information. I watched as students who were often unmotivated became eager to complete the Web site evaluations while they were in the lab. Most important, I saw students use both their time and the equipment efficiently for the entire period. With the exception of a few students who forgot to bring floppy disks on which to save their data, they all behaved like model students.

This time in the lab also provided one of those moments when the block period actually changes the learning environment so much that the role of the teacher changes as well. Instead of the usual "sage on the stage," in the computer lab, I truly functioned as their coach, helping them learn, practice, and hone their computer and information literacy skills. After I presented the goals for the day, there was very little for me to do but stand back and let them go at it. The students who knew how to use the Internet were off and running, while I helped the two or three groups that needed direct instruction. After the first 30 minutes I found myself getting bored, so I decided to watch over students' shoulders and ask them leading, thought-provoking questions. For example, I asked the students representing the Palestinian Authority if they had found a map detailing what parts of the occupied West Bank had been turned over to Palestinian control. I knew where they could find this data, so I was able to provide some general hints while still leaving the real search up to students.

In the last 30 minutes of the period, most students worked on their Web site evaluations. This provided another opportunity for me to interact with them in a different way. Recognizing that this task was tricky, some students actually asked me to watch them do the evaluations, an unusual request for any 16-year-old! Their ability to ask for help, and the luxury of having the time to sit down with small teams, made this period one of the most singularly pleasant days I had all year.

What kinds of rubrics can be employed to clarify expectations for students?

This question required me to focus on the various parts of the assignment that students had to complete. The project has four main elements: collecting information, evaluating the Web sites, synthesizing the data in a written position statement about each agenda issue, and oral debate and problem solving during the conference. The first two parts I choose to evaluate informally. Students who turned in a disk with all the required types of information received full credit. For the Web site evaluations, I focused on the annotation section rather than the rubric. Many students did a fairly superficial job on these and were disappointed by their scores. This poor performance clearly points to my failure to clarify the expectations. Although I told them what I expected for the annotation, I only covered it once in class and failed to provide any follow-up instructions or written models.

The last two parts of the assignment required more formal evaluation tools. The rubric for the agenda summaries was straightforward because we have used rubrics for various writing assignments throughout the course (see appendix F). I merely needed to decide what the focus should be. I chose to focus primarily on content, with a smaller portion of the score assigned to mechanics. This rubric was also much simpler than past ones because it basically worked as a checklist, without any gradations in score for judging quality. This made the tool effective for the teachers and simplified the expectations for students. On the whole, student performance on this section of the assignment led me to believe that this rubric was effective.

The other rubric had to evaluate both the quantity and quality of oral participation in the conference. With the extra time offered by the 100-minute period, students can get detailed feedback about their oral performance. After locking myself in the English office one afternoon, I was surprised to discover very little in the way of evaluation rubrics for speech among our curricular resources. The ones I did locate were based on debate competitions and relied too much on the teacher's subjective and personal judgment. I set out to take the best of what I found and create a system that not only would hold students accountable for participating during the conference, but also would provide a description of the quality of that participation. The tools I developed are the Participation Evaluation and Comments Log. The Participation Evaluation, the piece that determines the student's final score (see appendix G), includes a section for individual participation so students who participate less in oral activities can't completely hide behind their more outgoing teammates. There are six additional criteria for which team members are held jointly accountable:

- active cooperation by teams/individuals
- demonstrates use of speaking skills
- demonstrates knowledge
- balanced presentation
- appropriate discussion contributions
- overall frequency of contributions

The last two items could be observed and evaluated by the teacher, but instead I trained the Conference chairperson, a student, to record the frequency and style of comments, instead.

We used the Comments Log for this purpose (see appendix H). This form enabled me to set high expectations for participation that favored problem solving over debate. Each statement made by a team was recorded under one of five general categories:

- asks clarifying question
- specifically contradicts others
- provides information or opinion
- makes procedural statement
- makes inappropriate or unconstructive remarks

These styles of remarks fall along a continuum from most to least productive. Although I will probably change this form slightly next year, the initial results were far more favorable than I had hoped. Much to my amusement, I noticed many occasions where students prefaced a remark with a phrase like, "I want to pose a *clarifying question* to the country of. . . ." This kind of student focus on skills would have been less likely in a shorter period because the students would have felt that, with time short, it probably would be better to try to dominate other participants with more argumentative behavior.

Another by-product of this evaluation tool was an absence of behavior issues during the actual conference. Students were aware of the evaluations beforehand and had seen a demonstration during the mock conference session, so they were much more focused on problem solving than on debating. They were generally respectful of the student serving as chairperson. And while they did not always reach agreement or solve issues, many more issues were eventually resolved, and with much less rancor, than in previous years. In response to this dramatic change in participation, I will add another column titled, "makes proposal to resolve issue," to next year's Comments Log.

How can the United Nations Conference phase be restructured to encourage greater oral participation by all students? What is the impact of the 100-minute period on this kind of activity?

The answer to these two questions is simple. It's about *time*. We were able to provide more time than in previous years, for two reasons. First, we revised several sections of the course throughout the year in the hope that we could begin the Middle East unit two weeks earlier. While most of us only found an extra week, that was still a boost. More significant, restructuring the unit itself created more time. By letting the culminating activity, the simulation, drive instruction, it was easier to discard lessons that weren't relevant. In short, we did more with less.

The time of year was another factor. In previous years, students did not have a sense of the importance of the activity because I'd only used two block periods and one short period for the actual conference. In contrast, this year we had three block periods and two short periods. This greater time investment caused students to view the activity as more significant both in terms of their experience and their grade in the course.

Another way that time led me to restructure the activity was the use of 50 minutes of our block period for a mock conference. About a week and a half before the full conference began, I had students use the first agenda issue to practice the simulation. That is, they were taught about the procedures and methods of participating at the conference. We discussed parliamentary procedure and appropriate and inappropriate styles of participation. Next, I explained the details of the Participation Evaluation form. Students then made their opening remarks on the issue, and a short mock debate followed. The chairperson and I completed the Comments Log separately and compared our results afterward so we could norm the data and I could train the chairperson. In each class we had about 45 minutes for students to conduct their mock conference. Many students were surprised at how little was accomplished. They realized that we really would need a lot of time to actually resolve issues. For a majority of students this was also a wake-up call to pursue their research more diligently.

Another moment of discovery was the day during the conference that we had a short 35-minute period because of a school assembly. Students walked into the room with a totally different demeanor from their attitude the previous 100-minute period day. They expected to accomplish very little and did not involve themselves fully in oral participation. Some students appeared frustrated by the short period because they were eager to pick up where they had left off the previous day. Other students recognized that this time was insufficient to tackle an agenda issue and suggested using the period to meet "off the record" to negotiate with other countries on issues of their choice. These corridor discussions resulted in some interesting proposals over the next two periods of the conference. They also demonstrated the value students placed on the block period for this activity. I made a note in my own journal that this short period was useless. Next year I will follow the students' lead and purposely schedule some time for "off the record" negotiations. Having students reflect on the simulation would be another worthwhile activity for this day.

Parent Data

Parents' impressions of the research portion of the project were very positive. One parent's comment summarized the experience of most of the students: "At first, she said it was overwhelming, but later found it very educational and informative. Personally, I think it made her *think* and understand better the world around her. Is this really happening!?!"

Some parents cited difficulties in scheduling meetings between teammates, challenges when there was no Internet access at home, and a feeling that students were overwhelmed at first by the style of research and type of information being sought.

Parents were very supportive of the expectation that students rely on the Internet for their information. Only one parent voiced an objection to students relying solely on the Internet: "In order to be more realistic, students should utilize more sources of information besides the Internet." The following comments exemplify the response from all of the other parents on this issue:

- "This is a good example of the changes in obtaining information and the various tools students now have at their disposal. A sign of the times, but all to the good."
- "Just astounded that they go into the subjects in such depth. We appreciate that they got into the subjects in such depth. We appreciate the amount of work they do and the fact that it is made fun."
- "Gave them interesting perspective to the real-world issues, particularly because of having to represent one party in a conflict situation."
- "After observing him working on the Internet, I realized what an asset the Internet is to any research."
- "My child is now much more comfortable and skilled at using the Internet as an effective study/research tool. Discovering numerous Web sites and evaluating them are effective awareness exercises about the usefulness of the Internet."

These comments leave no doubt that Shorewood parents value the technology and information literacy skills taught in this unit.

In response to the question about students' use of time on the Internet, parents' opinions were as varied as the skill level of students in class. Parents whose children had previous experience using the Internet reported that students used their time efficiently. One said, "I was impressed that he was able to find much of the information on his own." Another parent demonstrated how important it is for the school to maintain its technological edge: "My daughter was able to take advantage of the technology at school to hasten the process." But a few parents pointed out that some students lacked adequate Internet research skills when they began the research. One parent noted that "at first his research on the Internet was barely adequate and he lacked some of the information he needed. By the later parts of the project he did find what he needed as his use of the Internet became sharper." This problem could be remedied if we spent a second period in the computer lab so that students who needed to develop their skills further could practice more advanced search strategies.

Another weakness in the simulation became manifest when I read the parent data. One parent wrote, " Her country's information was too limited. If she had been assigned a country that was more involved, her time would have been better spent." This student was assigned Libya. After watching the participants who represented Libya during the conference and conducting my own research on the Internet, I've decided to eliminate the country from next year's conference. This parent comment will also make me reevaluate how the Agenda Issues selection is written so that students who represent smaller, less documented nations such as Yemen and Oman receive more direction from the start. For example, there is a Web site about a regional desalination plant research project in Oman. Several of the students who represented Oman never located this site, so they did not have access to this information for the simulation. A lack of adequate information may have discouraged more active participation from these students.

Parents' perceptions of where students conducted their research may not be accurate, but these data provided some insights into student activity outside of class. The third section on the parent questionnaire asked them to report the percent of time students spent researching at a particular location. I was interested in where students reportedly spent a majority (50 percent or more) of their computer time. The results were:

- at home: 65 percent
- at partner's home: 12 percent
- at the Shorewood High library or in class: 14 percent
- at another library or site: 8 percent

I expected that students would rely more on school resources, so the importance of the home as the place to conduct research surprised me. But with such open-ended, time-intensive work, students recognized the benefits of working on their own at home. It may also be that students who already have Internet skills are more comfortable working on computers with which they are familiar. The reason for this student preference would be an interesting area for further study, especially as schools grapple with limited resources to apply to technology purchases.

Student Data

Overall, I was surprised by the maturity and insight of my students. In response to the question, "Why do you think I assigned this project?" most students articulated all or most of my own reasons. One student wrote:

> I think you had required us to only find sources from the Internet so that we could learn and practice our skills using the computer for future projects. The conference itself was to help us understand the complications of the issues in the Middle East and all the diverse opinions that clash with each other. We would especially learn a lot about the country that we represent during the conference. I also felt that the conference was done in this way for us to practice speech, debate, organization, and preparation skills, while representing our countries. It made us attempt to find a solution to issues even though we all had opposing ideas for each.

Another student explained the objectives succinctly:

> You assigned this project in order for us to: a) become proficient at using the Internet as a source of information; b) learn how to judge the value and validity of information on the web; c) develop the appropriate problem-solving skills to solve multifaceted conflicts; and d) learn in depth about the Middle East.

This kind of sophisticated description may indicate that the project was clearly defined, explained, organized, and taught-or it may simply mean that students are more aware of our intent than we think. Either way, it is gratifying that the students' and parents' explanations for the objectives behind the simulation so closely matched my own.

Students also contributed astute insights and critiques that will dictate future changes in these activities. A summary of these comments follows.

Introducing the assignment and initial research
(34 percent of students responded)

It was encouraging that students confirmed our decision to realign instruction to follow the topics covered by the conference agenda issues more explicitly. Several students remarked in this first set of reflections that the organization of the lessons helped with the research outside of class:

> I like what we are doing right now when we spend a whole class period and go in-depth about a different issue every day. After those classes I usually have a better understanding of the agenda issue, and it is easier for me to search for articles about it on the Internet.

Nevertheless, several students made constructive suggestions about how to use our 100-minute period to make their outside efforts more productive. One student noted that it was difficult to find time to coordinate information with his partner. His observations and suggestions directly relate to my research question concerning collaboration:

> We can use a 100-minute period to examine the sources that we already have, see how many agenda issues we have covered individually with those sources, and make lists of notes about what we then need to find in order to address all issues. Basically, a portion of the period, maybe 20 minutes, can be set aside for a reorganization to see what we have on each issue, and what then must be found so that we can become true representatives of our countries.

Another student echoed a comment I heard several times throughout the project:

> It would be really helpful if you would allow us more class time to use [the computers]. In this Internet time you could show us more Web site evaluations, including what you would consider a good vs. bad student evaluation. You could also focus more on shortcuts and estimating the value of different sites from the first screen. All in all though, I really feel like we should have more class time for the research of this project.

Although I reject the notion that more class time would automatically improve student performance, I agree that it is a good idea to reteach my expectations for the Web site evaluations. The next week I followed this student's other suggestion and demonstrated search strategies for news articles.

Mock conference day (32 percent of students responded)

This activity provided students with a taste of what the actual conference would be like, without the added stress of being graded. There were no data from this set of student responses specifically pertaining to the use of the block period. But students did make some comments that confirmed the importance of allowing them an ungraded trial run. One student wrote:

The biggest surprise was that no one seemed to be fully prepared for the conference at all. It seemed that we were basically running off of spontaneous, improvisational ideas as we went along.

In addition, students gave fair estimates about how much time would be required for discussion and resolution on each issue. Many students thought the conference would go quickly, but after the mock conference their revised estimates ran from 50 minutes to a full period for each issue. This new sense of timing probably helped students make more accurate judgments about how much the activity affected their grade and how to prepare more effectively.

Debate preparation (32 percent of students responded)

This set of questions asked students to reflect on their research work and the collegiality of their teams. Once again, students requested more class time to work with their partners, use computers in class, and consult with other student representatives. This last idea made immediate sense, and that time did get built into some sessions during the conference. The other common student comment concerned the use of time outside of class and the level of cooperation with partners. About 75 percent of the students who turned in this set of journals reported that they did their research independently, but then met with their partner periodically to share what they found. Some students also mentioned that after researching separately, they got together to write the conference agenda summaries. This independence was exactly what I'd hoped to discourage. Instead, by requiring nearly all research to be done outside of class, it seems that I fostered this individual approach to the work. Students did not offer any suggestions about how to improve this situation; in fact, they did not seem to feel it was a detriment to their performance.

In light of their actual practice and the parents' comments about difficulties with conflicting schedules, I may have to accept that there is no way to control for this absence of teamwork. The fact that some students wrote that they met before the conference sessions began is encouraging. More important, I must keep in mind that teamwork during the conference was my ultimate goal. There was an explicit section on one of the evaluation tools (see appendix G) used during the conference sessions that held students accountable for this teamwork. Using the block period to provide more opportunities for team research may improve the situation, but it may be more realistic for teachers to give up attempting to influence research styles outside the classroom setting.

Mid-simulation (27 percent of students responded)

At this stage, my primary interest was students' responses to the question, "What could we do with a 100-minute period to make the actual conference debate/discussion more effective?" The responses did not convey a need for dramatic changes. But they did demonstrate that revising the instructional strategies that led up to the conference encouraged students to focus on problem solving the agenda issues rather than winning debates. Here are some sample comments:

- "If we were to have a few minutes before each class to meet with other nations, we could have more thoughtful, better planned proposals."
- "I propose that there should be a 20-minute period in which we could strike deals with other countries. All we would need to do is start the conference earlier in the year, and this plan would work."
- "Mr. Sherman could discuss with us, as a class, what we could have proposed or done in order to attain peace; sort of like a conclusion to each day's discussions."

The idea that I have some magic solution to all the conflicts in the Middle East amuses me. Nevertheless, these comments demonstrate that students went beyond the debate style approach I'd observed in previous years and entered the simulation with a more sophisticated goal.

These statements also point to a need for students to reflect on their experience, which is possible with the 100-minute period. It will simply take an active effort on the teacher's part to include it. This kind of reflection could be written and graded formally, or it could consist of an informal class discussion. In either case, it is important to provide students with some opportunity to explore and recognize the larger learning that take place during the actual conference.

Postsimulation (21 percent of students responded)

Here I was interested primarily in students' thoughts about collaboration. The final question asked them how they could work better with their partner. Although a few students thought they demonstrated excellent teamwork, many of the comments I received reiterated the need for teams to work more closely during the research phase:

- "After the entire project was finished, I realized that how well you work with your partner would significantly affect the result of the project. One way to work better with your partner is to schedule the time with him or her in advance, to share and discuss your ideas and information."
- "I think the only way that my partner and I could have worked better would have been if we both did research on the Internet and not just the person who had home access. This would have helped us to do a better job on our [written] summaries because we didn't seem to find the information we needed, and were vigorously looking for, until after we turned the summaries in. This worked to our disadvantage and could have been prevented by using the skills I have now, but didn't have then."
- "In terms of having fun and getting along, we had no problem. But we weren't too efficient in time management. Often, in the midst of deadlines, we would

find ourselves watching television or playing basketball. One way to offset this would be to work at a neutral site like school, not one of our homes. That way we wouldn't be distracted by other things."

This last, honest comment about wasting time leads me to wonder how the block period could be used specifically to teach the time management skills that all teachers desire of their students. A 100-minute period is a chunk of time that more realistically mimics the workplace, so perhaps some lessons could focus directly on using time efficiently. Though I like to think my classroom is run as efficiently as possible, students may lack models of workplace behaviors that would help them stay focused when they work in teams outside of class. Perhaps these behaviors could be made more explicit in a second class period at the computer lab.

Action Plan

Many of the revisions that I will implement are sprinkled throughout my findings. Here is a summary of the changes I will make to the simulation and my instructional practices.

First, I will revise the simulation itself. In the course of the year we will expand the list of resources linked from our Web site so that students have more direction and structure as they begin their research. Second, Libya will be removed from the list of countries. The Agenda Issues will be revised so that, where appropriate, they mention the smaller, less known nations in the region.

As for instruction, I will plan for a second full period in the computer lab to work further with students on their technology skills. I will also clarify the expectations for the annotations on the Web Site Evaluation form and reteach this skill throughout the research phase.

In terms of the block period, I will take further advantage of the flexibility it offers by scheduling more short, 20-minute activities. These will include more demonstrations of Internet search strategies and evaluations of Web sites. I will also seek out lessons that teach time management skills specifically, especially in the context of teamwork. During the research phase I will provide two or three 10-minute blocks of time for teammates to share their findings and coordinate their schedules.

Finally, I will try to carve out similar short blocks of time during the conference itself. Some of these mini-blocks will provide students with time to reassess their strategies and meet informally with representatives from other nations. More important, I will create some tools for encouraging students to reflect on their experiences at the conference and their larger lessons from the research and simulation. Through their engagement in such reflection, I will encourage students to end this simulation with a larger understanding of international relations, conflict resolution, and the complexities facing their future world.

Appendix A

United Nations Conference on Middle East Peace and Development

Instructions and Research Guide

http://schools.shorelineschools.org/shorewood/Academics/ss/ws10/MESim/default.html

You are going to represent a country at a United Nations Conference on Middle East Peace and Development. Please research the country that you have been assigned and the issues on the *Conference Agenda*. To prepare, your goal is to be as familiar as possible with your country and the issues on the Agenda. You will be graded on

- individual research
- oral participation and behavior at the conference
- how realistically you represent your country
- your demonstrated understanding of the Agenda issues

The following countries may be present at the Conference. Please circle the country that you have been assigned to represent.

Egypt	Kuwait	Saudi Arabia
Iran	Lebanon	Syria
Iraq	Libya	Turkey
Israel	Oman	United Arab Emirates
Jordan	Palestinian Authority*	Yemen

* The permanent status of the West Bank and Gaza Strip are subject to further negotiation. At this time, the Palestinian Authority has observer status at the United Nations, no voting rights, and is not a recognized state.

Be sure to ask any questions about the *Conference Agenda* issues before the Conference begins. Remember that you are at the Conference to serve your country in the best possible way. This may not always mean doing what is best for other countries in the area. On the other hand, when you negotiate for your country you may want to consider the benefits of a lasting peace and cooperation between the countries of the Middle East. Some questions to consider:

- Who are your allies? Who are your historical enemies?
- Who are your most important trading partners?
- What is your military status?
- What benefit or harm will be caused to your government or your nation's people if an agenda issue is decided one way or another?
- For which agenda issues can you take a leadership role at the conference?

• Are there any other nations you may want to work with to present proposals?

Activities and Assignments

A. Create two large (8½ × 11 inch) maps of your country, both of which should include seven basic parts of a map, and label countries that are immediate neighbors. Each partner must make one map.

   • Political map; label all major cities, roads, and waterways
   • "Physical" map showing economic data of your choice\

B. Each team will turn in a PowerMac readable disk with the following documents saved in text only format. Along with your disk include a single sheet of paper listing the contents. For #3 (government documents) and #4 (articles) below, indicate which *Conference Agenda Issue* is addressed.

   1. Any two of the following United States government publications:
      • *CIA World Factbook*
      • U.S. State Department *Background Notes*
      • Library of Congress *Country Studies*
   2. One "biased" information data source about your country
   3. Three government documents pertaining to any *Conference Agenda* issues
   4. Five electronically based news articles that:
      • refer to a *Conference Agenda* issue
      • are about your country or written from its perspective
      • indicate source and date of the article

C. Complete evaluations (a rubric and criteria will be discussed and distributed separately) for six of your Internet sources. Do not evaluate the overall site, instead aim for a specific Web page that refers to one of the *Conference Agenda Issues*. Evaluate . . .
   • one "biased" information data source
   • three of the government documents
   • two of the news articles
   NOTE: Do **not** evaluate the CIA World *Factbook* or State Department *Background Notes* or the Library of Congress *Country Studies*.

The evaluation criteria and a sample evaluation rubric are located at:
http://www.shorelin.wednet.edu/shorewood/departments/ss/ws10/MESim/Web_eval.html

D. Write a *three*-page (minimum) summary of your country's position on each of

the issues and proposals on the *Conference Agenda Issues*.
A draft of your summary is due:
The final version of your summary is due:

E. Make a large name tag for your country that will be placed at your country's table during the Conference.

Appendix B

Conference Agenda Issues

ISSUE 1—Proposal

Syria proposes that Israel be expelled from the conference and that the goals of the conference be redirected toward establishing a pan-Islamic organization that would unite all Islamic nations both spiritually and politically. This proposal would radically change the conference's goals of reducing tension in the area. The newly proposed organization would replace or strengthen the current Islamic Conference Organization. If the proposal is adopted, then the United States has threatened to cut off military and economic aid to Egypt, Jordan, Lebanon, Oman, Saudi Arabia, Turkey, and Kuwait. The European Community has made no official statement regarding this proposal.

ISSUE 2

In 1967 Israel occupied land belonging to Egypt, Syria, and Jordan, including the Old City of Jerusalem. Under the Camp David Accords of 1978, Israel agreed to negotiate a settlement with Egypt that would lead to some kind of autonomous rule for Palestinians in the Gaza Strip and the West Bank of the Jordan River. The exact nature of this Palestinian self-rule is still not finalized, and negotiations with the Palestinian Authority continue. One major sticking point in these negotiations remains the dispute over control of the city of Jerusalem. Final settlement of the status of the Israeli-occupied territories and Jerusalem should be a goal of the conference.

ISSUE 3—Proposal

An official statement of policy should be created that will announce a unified declaration denouncing terrorism as a means of settling disputes. All members who ratify this statement should then decide on methods of enforcement. These methods may include, but are not limited to, airport and seaport inspection, multinational security teams, exchange of intelligence information to track down terrorist groups, and a regional court to decide cases regarding alleged terrorist acts. This proposal is made jointly by Egypt and Israel with support from several European states and the United States.

ISSUE 4

Iran is distressed that the other Islamic nations in the region have begun to lose traditional Islamic values and allowed "Western" ideas to infiltrate all levels of society. Saudi Arabia feels that a reinterpretation of Islamic law must be made in order to function in a global environment where its oil is required for existence. Some nations in the region agree with Saudi Arabia, but fear revolution by Islamic fundamentalists.

ISSUE 5

One of the ongoing disputes that divides the region concerns water resources. There are conflicts surrounding the use of water from the Tigris, Euphrates, and Jordan rivers. In addition, the Aswan High Dam has created environmental problems for Egyptian farmers. Israel would like to share its technological developments in low water agriculture and desalination plants in return for closer economic ties with its neighbors. A statement of interregional policy for coping with water resources in light of increasing population demands and a plan technology sharing should be addressed.

ISSUE 6

Some of the nations in the region do not have very large oil reserves. They would like to set up a fund in which 2 percent of the GNP of the larger oil-producing countries would be distributed for economic development in their countries. This development would include industry and agriculture. Furthermore, the oil rich nations will sell oil at a 15 percent reduction in price to those Middle Eastern nations that do not produce enough oil to meet their own needs.

ISSUE 7

Despite an end to the civil war of the 1970s and '80s, the situation in Lebanon remains unstable. Syria occupies most of the northern and eastern parts of the nation, while Israeli-backed Christian militiamen dominate the southern portion of the country. The government's attempts to maintain internal peace continue to be hampered by infighting among various religious and political factions. The political governing of Lebanon has most recently been dominated by Syria. Israel and some other nations in the area want to restrict Syria's power in Lebanon because they believe that Syria ultimately wants to annex Lebanon. Syria has defended its position by asserting that it is the only nation in the area that can adequately insure peace and reduce Israeli intervention in Lebanon.

Appendix C

World Wide Web Evaluation Standards
(Adapted from Elizabeth Kirk's Evaluating Information Found on the Internet.)

There are no filters between you and the Internet. The ease of constructing Web documents results in information of the widest range of quality, written by authors of the widest range of authority, available on a level playing field. Excellent resources reside alongside the most dubious. The Internet epitomizes the concept of *Caveat lector*: Let the reader beware!

All information, whether in print or by byte, needs to be evaluated by readers for authority, appropriateness, and other personal criteria for value. Never use information that you cannot verify. Establishing and learning criteria to filter information you find on the Internet is a good beginning for becoming a critical consumer of information in all forms. Cast a cold eye (as Yeats wrote) on everything you read. Question it. Look for other sources that can authenticate or corroborate what you find. Learn to be skeptical and then learn to trust your instincts.

Site Home Page

Look at the web page you are trying to evaluate. Does it include any of the following?

- A header or footer that shows its affiliation as part of a larger Web site.
- A watermark or wallpaper that fulfills the same function.
- A link that allows you to send a message to the site Webmaster.

These features help you judge the "official character" of a web page. They act as an assurance that the page you are evaluating functions within some type of institutional setting. Judging the official nature of a web page is extremely important if the page is not signed. Some Web sites do not include attributions to individual authors, so you will have to rely on your ability to evaluate the institution, or domain, where the page lives.

- Can you find the Web site's home page by deleting all the information in the URL after the server name?
- Can you tell if the page is actually part of someone's personal account, as opposed to being part of an official site? Click "url.html" for help in evaluating this kind of URL.

Poor:

- The page is part of someone's personal Internet account.

Fair:

- The page contains a link that allows you to send a message to the site Web-master.
- After searching, you found the publisher's name, but do not have enough information to judge its reputation as an information source.

Good:

- The page contains header or footer that shows its affiliation as part of a larger Web site.
- The page contains watermark or wallpaper that fulfills the same function.
- The page contains a link at the bottom or top that allows you to go to the home page of the Web site where the document lives.
- The site resides within some institutional setting that is recognized in the field in which you are studying.

Best:

- The name of the organization is given on the document you are reading.
- There are headers, footers, or a distinctive watermark that *clearly* show the document to be part of an official academic or scholarly Web site.
- This organization is recognized in the field in which you are studying.

Searchability

Poor:

- Neither the page nor the Web site contains an index or search engine.

Fair:

- The site contains its own index, but the index does not use active links.
- There is no search engine for this Web site.
- You could not easily locate additional information buried under several layers of pages

Good:

- The site and/or page contains an index that uses active links.
- You could easily locate additional information buried under several layers of pages.

Best:

- In addition to Good above, the Web site contains its own search engine.

Authorship of Article within a Site

What do we need to know about the author? When the author is someone unknown to you, ask the following questions:

1. Is the document signed?
2. Can I get more information on the author by linking from this page to other documents?
3. Was there information about the author on the page from which I linked to this one?

    If you can answer "Yes" to the second or third question, it's possible that you will have enough information to judge who the author is. You may also be able to find the author's telephone number or e-mail address so that you may contact him or her with questions.

Poor:

- The document is unsigned and not directly associated with a relevant institution or organization.

Fair:

- The document is unsigned, but you found or linked to the page from another document or Web site you trust.
- There is an address and telephone number as well as an e-mail address for the author in order to request further information on his or her work and professional background.

Good:

- The document is signed, but you had to look elsewhere for the author's scholarly or professional affiliation.
- The document is unsigned, but can be trusted because the publisher is clearly indicated and is a reputable source.

Best:

- The document is signed by an author with scholarly or professional affiliation with a relevant institution or organization.

Quality of Information

Poor:

- The information provided does not relate to the topic you are researching.
- The reading level of the site is not appropriate for your use.
- The site does not include links to other relevant information.

Fair:

- The information provided relates somewhat to the topic you are researching.
- The reading level of the site is not appropriate for your use.
- The site does not include links to other relevant information.

Good:

- The information provided mostly relates to the topic you are researching.
- The reading level of thc site is appropriate for your use.
- The site does not include links to other relevant information.

Best:

- The information provided relates specifically to the topic you are researching.
- The reading level of the site is appropriate for your use.
- The site includes links to other relevant information.

Timeliness

(of the Web site or document itself)

Poor:

- There is no indication of a date at the web site, on the Web page, or in the document.

Fair:

- The "Document info" feature in the "View" menu on Netscape tells you the date of the page.
- There is no other indication of the date of the specific information on the page and/or document.

Good:

- The page includes information within the document, like a caption, that indicates currency.
- If the page contains statistics, the source is captioned or listed in a bibliography for the page.

Best:

- There is clear indication of the currency of the specific information on the page and/or document.
- The page or Web site contains a "last updated" date.

Distractions

Poor:

- The site contains links to games, chat rooms, or other sites not associated with the assignment.
- The site contains inappropriate advertising and/or graphics.

Fair:

- The site is heavily graphic in nature, resulting in a delay in viewing information.
- The site contains some advertising.

Good:

- The site contains graphics in limited amounts that do not significantly delay viewing.
- The site contains very little advertising.

Best:

- The site contains minimal graphics that enhance the information or usefulness of the page.
- The site contains no advertising.

World Wide Web Site Evaluation Form

Name of Site: _____ Agenda Issue: _____

Internet Address: http:// _____

Your name: _____

Refer to the "World Wide Web Evaluation Standards" handout to complete this form.

	Poor	Fair	Good	Best
Site Home Page	2	3	4	5
Searchability	2	3	4	5
Authorship of Article within a Site	2	3	4	5
Quality of Information	2	3	4	5
Timeliness	2	3	4	5
Distractions	2	3	4	5

Annotation:

Appendix D

Student Journals

Middle East Simulation Action Research Project

Extra Credit Available: 25 points possible

As you and your parents are aware, I am conducting research to analyze the use of 100-minute periods throughout the Middle East Simulation Project. Your insights into the assignment and activities are essential data for helping me to understand the activity. I need your help, therefore, to complete a special, separate "journal" in which you reflect on your work throughout the simulation.

Students who complete all or part of this assignment and turn it in separately will receive credit. Please use separate paper for each journal entry and be sure to write your name and period and title the entry. Each response is worth one extra credit point. Journal entries must be written within the time frame listed and are due on the date noted. (No extensions are possible.)

The criteria for awarding points is simple. For credit you must

- answer in complete sentences
- write legibly or type
- title each separate assignment using the boldfaced headings below
- provide responses that demonstrate mature, reflective thinking

A. **Introducing the assignment and initial research** 7 pts. possible, due Friday, May 22

1. Why do you think I assigned this project?
2. What are you interested in or excited about?
3. What do you anticipate will be the most challenging aspect of the assignment?
4. How have you and your partner been working so far? Do you work together, separately, divide work, or one person does it all?
5. Have you found information directly related to the Agenda Issues?
6. What could we do with a 100-minute period to make the research you do outside of class more effective?

B. **Mock conference day** 5 pts. possible, Period 4: due Thursday, May 28; Periods 1 & 3: due Friday, May 29

1. How well did you accomplish your goals today?

2. Were you able to solve problems, or did you simply argue with other delegates?

3. Were there any surprises? Explain.

4. How much time do you think we will need to cover the remaining issues?

5. What will you and your partner do to prepare for the next sessions?

C. **Debate Preparation** 4 pts. possible, Periods 1 & 3: due Monday, June 8; Period 4: due Tuesday, June 9

1. How did you and your partner collaborate? Did you work together, separately, divide work, or one person did it all?

2. Based on the preparation work you have done so far, predict your success at the Conference in terms of

   a. your active, vocal contributions to the discussions

   b. your ability to negotiate successfully and accomplish some of your nation's goals.

   c. Why would you make those predictions?

3. What Agenda items were most difficult for you to prepare for?

4. What could we do with a 100-minute period to make the research you do outside of class more effective?

D. **Mid-simulation** 5 pts. possible, Periods 1 & 3: due Wednesday, June 10; Period 4: due Friday, June 12

1. How much time do you think we will need to cover the remaining issues?

2. How well did you accomplish your nation's goals so far?

3. Were you able to solve problems, or did you argue with other delegates?

4. Were there any surprises? Explain.

5. What could we do with a 100-minute period to make the actual Conference debate/discussion more effective?

E. **Post-simulation** 5 pts. possible, Periods 1 & 3: **due in my box** Tuesday, June 16; Period 4: **due in class** Wednesday, June 17

1. Why do you think I assigned this project?

2. How well did you accomplish your nation's goals?

3. What would you have done differently to

   a. increase your level of participation?

   b. have a more successful outcome for your nation?

   c. work better with your partner?

NOTE: If you miss a deadline, the work will not be counted. Please be sure to carefully meet all deadlines for credit.

Appendix E

Parent Questionnaire

Action Research Project

As you are aware, I am conducting research to analyze the use of the 100-minute period throughout the Middle East Simulation Project. Your insights into the assignment and activities are essential data for helping me to understand the activity. I am particularly interested in getting a sense of the collegiality students demonstrated in working together on their research.

   NOTE: There will be a box provided in class to turn in this form so your responses remain anonymous. Thank you for taking the time to complete the following questions.

David Sherman
Shorewood Social Studies Department

1. Do you have Internet access at home? _____ Yes   _____ No

2. Do you feel that you were in a position to directly observe your child as he/she conducted the research for this project? _____ Yes   _____ No

3. About what percent of your child's research time was spent
    _____ at home?
    _____ at his/her partner's home?
    _____ at the Shorewood library/in class?
    _____ at another library?
    _____ other?
    (Is the total 100?)

4. What was your child's attitude toward this project?

5. What was your child's attitude toward working with a partner?

6. How did this attitude compare to other projects where he/she had a partner?

7. How effective was your child's use of time on the Internet?

8. What is your overall reaction to the research portion of the project?

Appendix F

Conference Agenda Issues Summary Evaluation

Name(s): _____   _____

Score: _____ / ___ points

	not yet at standard	achieves standard
Agenda Issue 1 Score: ___ / 5		
– clear and concise writing that summarizes main points	0	1
– logical use of factual evidence	0	1
– nation's point of view presented realistically	0	1
– fully developed paragraph	0	1
– mechanics (spelling, punctuation, capitalization,	0	1
– grammar, and use of complete sentences)		
Agenda Issue 2 Score: ___ / 5		
– clear and concise writing that summarizes main points	0	1
– logical use of factual evidence	0	1
– nation's point of view presented realistically	0	1
– fully developed paragraph	0	1
– mechanics	0	1
Agenda Issue 3 Score: ___ / 5		
– clear and concise writing that summarizes main points	0	1
– logical use of factual evidence	0	1
– nation's point of view presented realistically	0	1
– fully developed paragraph	0	1
– mechanics	0	1
Agenda Issue 4 Score: ___ / 5		
– clear and concise writing that summarizes main points	0	1
– logical use of factual evidence	0	1
– nation's point of view presented realistically	0	1
– fully developed paragraph	0	1
mechanics	0	1

Score: _____ / ___ points	not yet at standard	achieves standard
Agenda Issue 5 Score: ___ / 5		
– clear and concise writing that summarizes main points	0	1
– logical use of factual evidence	0	1
– nation's point of view presented realistically	0	1
– fully developed paragraph	0	1
– mechanics	0	1
Agenda Issue 6 Score: ___ / 5		
– clear and concise writing that summarizes main points	0	1
– logical use of factual evidence	0	1
– nation's point of view presented realistically	0	1
– fully developed paragraph	0	1
– mechanics	0	1
Agenda Issue 7 Score: ___ / 5		
– clear and concise writing that summarizes main points	0	1
– logical use of factual evidence	0	1
– nation's point of view presented realistically	0	1
– fully developed paragraph	0	1
– mechanics	0	1

Appendix G

U.N. Conference Participation Evaluation

(Group and/or Individual Score)

Name(s): _____   Name _____

Score: _____ /60   Score: _____ /60

Individual Participation:

	below	at			below	at
none	standard	standard		none	standard	standard
0	7	10		0	7	10

– stayed focused and on task   – stayed focused and on task
– prepared each day   – prepared each day
– spoke at least once each day   – spoke at least once each day
– did not miss any days   – did not miss any days

"Team" Participation:

	no cooperation	not very active	active	highly active
Active cooperation by teams/individuals: – assisted partner to use notes, articles, summary – consulted partner before addressing the group	0	7	9	10

	not demonstrated	below standard	mostly at standard	exceeds standard
Demonstrates use of speaking skills: – clear, convincing speech – direct eye contact with class	0	7	9	10

	not demonstrated	below standard	mostly at standard	exceeds standard
Demonstrates knowledge: – of the nation you represent – of the Conference Agenda Issues – of your allies and enemies	0	7	9	10

	unrealistic and uncooperative	realistic **or** cooperative	realistic **and** cooperative
Balanced presentation: – clearly stated your country's interests/opinions – cooperated with nations on common concerns	3	4	5

	mostly inappropriate remarks	mostly appropriate remarks	used a variety of appropriate remarks

Appropriate discussion contributions:
 – to be evaluated at the end of
   the conference based on the
   "Conference Comments Log"
	6	8	10

	infrequent remarks	average remarks	frequent remarks

Overall frequency of contributions:
 – to be evaluated at the end of
   the conference based on the
   "Conference Comments Log"
	3	4	5

Appendix H

Participation Comments Log

Conference Chair _____ Agenda Issue # _____

	asks clarifying question	specifically contradicts others	provides information or opinion	makes procedural statement	makes inappropriate or unconstructive remarks
Egypt					
Iran					
Iraq					
Israel					
Jordan					
Kuwait					
Lebanon					
Libya					
Oman					
Palestinian Authority					
Saudi Arabia					
Syria					
Turkey					
United Arab Emirates					
Yemen					

5

Teaching Work World Components in the High School Science Classroom

Tracy Stoops
Shorewood High School

Tracy Stoops, a high school biology teacher who was planning a new course in biotechnology, wanted to investigate to what extent and in what ways the 100-minute block period facilitated the integration of *work world components* into high school science classes. She identified three such components—the use of job shadows, the engagement of working scientists in the activities of the high school science classroom, and the use of labs that simulated workplace research activities—and researched their use in her biology classes. She found that each of these *work world components* was supported in its instructional application by 100-minute block periods.

Introduction and Research Question

Our most recent focus at Shorewood High School (described in chapter 1) has been examining and implementing the Washington State Essential Academic Learning Requirements, a statewide, legislatively mandated set of curriculum standards defining what each student must know and be able to do at grade levels 4, 7, and 10. One category of objectives described in the Essential Learning Requirements is what I term *work world components*. These components include skills a student needs to be a successful beginning employee in a particular workplace, relevant knowledge a student wants regarding the activities in a workplace and the expectations of a new employee, and some experience for a student in an actual work situation, such as a job shadow or internship.

One example of the integration of these work world components into a high school class is the weaving of child care information, insights, and skills into a family science course. In such a course students learn about human development in childhood, the needs and capacities of young children in particular, and the issues and challenges involved in caring for young children. Students also have opportunities arranged by the teacher to discuss child care issues with child care professionals and parents who use child care, and they visit child care centers to observe. Finally, students bring their knowledge and incipient skills together, perhaps first by job shadowing a child caregiver and then by serving an internship at a child care facility.

Many vocational classes at Shorewood include these kinds of work world components—for example, marketing, drafting, auto mechanics, and wood shop courses. Even before we implemented the Essential Academic Learnings, the Shorewood community valued work world skills and experience, as illustrated by our somewhat unusual graduation requirement that every student successfully complete at least one year of a vocational course that meets the state requirements for the vocational designation:

- The instructor of any such course must be vocationally certified, which requires at least 2,000 hours of paid work experience in the field.
- The class must be approved by the state's Office of the Superintendent of Public Instruction (OSPI—the Washington equivalent of the state department of education), which must establish a proven need for workers in that field.
- There must be a school-focused advisory group that includes representatives from local colleges and businesses, similar programs in other districts, and the community at large.
- The class itself must belong to a local organization that promotes education about the specific vocation being taught.

Within this context of a long-standing commitment to high-quality vocational education, Shorewood recently applied to the OSPI for permission to offer a vocationally approved course in biotechnology. Our application was approved, and the course will be offered next fall for the first time. This course will enrich the science department 's offerings by providing a science class that relates directly to the work world—specifically, the laboratory field. The biotechnology course will provide an exciting opportunity for students to obtain vocational credit in a nontraditional vocational course that will inspire students heading to college and provide them with entry-level workplace skills that will enable them to work in labs in the biotech industry while they continue their formal education. The course will include a variety of topics, such as immunology, microbiology, media preparation, gel electrophoresis, DNA sequencing and synthesis, protein identification, independent research opportunities, and job shadowing. Prerequisites for this course include biology and chemistry, or biology with chemistry taken simultaneously with the biotechnology course. In addition, because of the academic nature of the course, it will be cross-credited with the science department, and students will be able to take the course for either vocational or science lab credit. In sum, with the push for school-to-work opportunities, and with the Essential Learnings placing a greater focus on preparing students for careers, this class provides a welcome new opportunity for the college-motivated student to complete a vocational class and gain useful job skills.

As the instructor of this new course in biotechnology, I found myself wondering how the current Shorewood daily schedule will lend itself to this biotechnology class. Shorewood has had block periods for the past four years using an "ABC" schedule. Each block period is 100 minutes long. To be specific, *I wanted to investigate in what ways and to what extent 100-minute block periods are conducive to integrating work world components into the curricula of our current science courses.* Of course, my motive was to gather relevant insights and guidelines from this research that I can apply to my planning for the biotechnology course.

Description of Research

To address this question I looked at three different *work world components* provided for students in current biology classes, because I hope to use and probably expand each of these in the new biotechnology course. These three components are:

- *the experience component:* a job shadow, in which a student visits a workplace and follows an employee at the facility for a given length in her/his work life; or an internship, in which a student works at a facility as an aide or assistant.
- *the knowledge component:* enhancing students' knowledge of the work world by bringing practitioners in the field into the high school classroom so students can hear from and interact with them. This includes presentations by visiting scientists and their assistance with complicated labs.
- *the skill-building component:* students conduct laboratory experiments in the high school classroom that simulate current biotechnology research experiences enabling the students to develop the skills needed in the laboratory workplace.

Component One: *The Experience Component—*
Experiences in the Work Place: Job Shadows or Internships

The first of these three components, with a focus in this situation on job shadowing, had the most straightforward response to the role of 100-minute periods on the activity. Forty-five Shorewood teachers from various subject areas and 33 students from my honors biology class were asked the same question: "Are longer periods of 100 minutes more conducive to job shadow opportunities for you/your students? Why?" The results were tallied and recorded. In this survey, the results were overwhelmingly supportive of 100-minute periods. A total of only three students and teachers thought that the daily schedule had no impact on the ease of participating in a job shadow experience. All of the rest thought the 100-minute periods were better.

Reasons for this stemmed largely from the fact that there are only three periods on most days in our schedule. So if a job shadow experience required a student to miss a day of school, only two classes besides the biotechnology course would be missed, and the impact on the student's work in other classes would be minimized. Also, it would be possible to schedule the job shadow for some students around the lunch hour. The student would then have approximately 150 minutes to participate in a job shadow and might not need to miss any other classes.

Teachers and students alike felt that job shadowing was a very valuable workplace experience for a vocational program. As one student explained, "I found my job shadow to be more informative and helpful in [teaching me] how a laboratory is conducted than experiences provided in the course." After reading the student surveys and reviewing the positive attitudes of students and faculty about the opportunities for job shadows provided by our block schedule, I believe that each student in this vocational course must be provided with a job shadow opportunity. In this course, the nature of the subject requires that the job shadow take place in a laboratory setting. Experience in real laboratories will provide students with immediate connections, both academic and experiential, to the work world of science.

While this study has confirmed my belief in the need to include job shadowing experiences in the new vocational biotechnology course, I also want to explore the possibility of offering laboratory internship experiences to some or all of the students in this class. It seems to me that internships, which would be longer and more engaging, would provide students with an even richer and more challenging work world experience.

Component Two: *The Knowledge Component—* ### Involving Scientists in the Classroom

The second component, involving scientists from the work world in the high school classroom to assist students with challenging labs and to give presentations, was already in place in several units of the honors biology curriculum. These lessons, focusing on DNA synthesis, DNA sequencing, and bioethics, were developed by Shorewood teachers in collaboration with Dr. Maureen Munn at the University of Washington's Division of Molecular Biotechnology. Part of this project was to enlist science researchers in helping teachers to complete some of the more complicated lab procedures and help troubleshoot problems that developed as we adapted the labs for high school use. These scientists, who worked with Dr. Munn as graduate students, were engaged with students in several different ways—for example, helping with complicated procedures such as running the biotechnology equipment, helping students to develop their own research questions, and showing students how to follow up the initial data they had collected with research inquiries. Some of the scientists also agreed to participate at the end of the unit as guest lecturers, sharing their work experiences and career paths with the high school students.

I found the services offered by these scientists to be a tremendous benefit for my students, and I know that these interactions provided my students with contacts in the workplace that they otherwise would not have. The developer of this curriculum, Maureen Munn, indicated in her questionnaire (see appendix C) that she also agreed strongly that the hands-on involvement of scientists was crucial to the success of the program.

To ascertain whether the scientists' involvement in a biotechnology classroom is a valuable work world component, and to determine if our block period schedule makes this participation more feasible for scientists, I surveyed the scientists (see appendix D) and students (see appendix A). I expected that both the students and the scientists would find this experience to be valuable, and that the 100-minute period would be seen as beneficial by these traveling scientists. But I received some surprising responses.

The 53 students who were surveyed rated the following statement on a 1 (strongly disagree) to 4 (strongly agree) scale: *It is important for students to have scientists assist with and answer questions during these lessons.* The average student response was 3.16, indicating clear support for this position. The students' rating of the value of the scientists' role, however, was not as strong as that of the teachers and program developers, who all rated this statement as 4. The reasons for this discrepancy may be that students are inexperienced at developing good science curriculum and may not be as conscious of the effort and time that goes into making these connections or the true value of such connections, or they may have experienced a visiting scientist who was less able to relate to them than some of the more engaging visitors. In spite of this variation in response, both students and teachers on the whole found the visiting scientists to be valuable elements in the learning experience.

As for the visiting scientists, six were asked the following multiple-choice question:

> I think the most valuable part of this lesson for students that would help
> them appreciate the work world is:
> a. information provided by the teacher.
> b. hands-on experience in the lab.
> c. cooperative group work required for this lab.
> d. the chance to question and work with scientists (appendix D).

Of the three who circled choice (d), two also selected (b), and one also chose (b) and (c). The other three selected choice (b) alone. This set of responses suggests that the scientists on the whole viewed their role more as one of support for the hands-on lab experience, and that they saw the hands-on lab work as providing the core of work world experience. Of course, half of them also viewed their role as being directly related to this goal.

Given the fact that teachers, students, and the scientists themselves saw the scientists' participation as valuable to work world learning, I will strive to strengthen the connections we have built in this direction and expand on the types and numbers of scientists participating in current science projects and in the new biotechnology course.

The involvement of scientists should not replace the teacher's role, however. As one student commented in the student survey, "Teachers are far better then professionals [scientists] at explaining things." This statement may or may not be true in any particular context, depending on what is being explained. I think the point of this comment is that teachers are experienced in teaching high school science; they know the students and their learning styles, and they have taught the course up to the introduction of these work world labs. Therefore, the teachers need to be involved as partners with the visiting scientists because the teachers are the professionals when it comes to teaching high school students.

Finally, all six visiting scientists commented that it didn't seem to make a difference in student learning how long the class was on the days they attended. However, with our current schedule, the laboratory experiments are done in two 100-minute periods and one 50-minute period. If we had the traditional schedule of 50-minute class periods, these labs would need to meet every day, and the visiting scientists would need to attend more days in a row—specifically, five days instead of three. I believe that it is reasonable to assume that being away from their regular jobs on so many consecutive days would make it more difficult for the scientists to become involved in these activities. So, it seems evident to me that 100-minute periods made it more likely that these scientists could be involved in the classroom and would choose to do so.

Component Three: *The Skill-Building Component*—
Lab Activities that Simulate the Workplace and Increase Student Skills

This component focused on integrating laboratory activities into the curriculum that were a close simulation of laboratory activities currently underway in the workplace. My questions for study were these:

> How well can classroom lab activities designed for this purpose actually simulate a work world laboratory?

> To what extent and in what ways does the 100-minute block period support the effectiveness and value of such labs?

Creating realistic lab simulations presents challenges to the high school science teacher. First of all, such labs require years to develop and depend on the cooperation of scientists in the field who are current in many aspects of laboratory techniques. In addition, because of the nature of biotechnology and laboratory work, the expense is usually beyond what a school district can afford for a science classroom.

We at Shorewood High School are very fortunate in having an excellent support system from our local universities and research facilities. The Department of Molecular Biotechnology at the University of Washington (UW) in Seattle was provided with funding through the federal government's Human Genome Project to work with K–12 educators. Dr. Maureen Munn of the UW Molecular Biotechnology Division heads up the education program for the high school portion of the Human Genome Project. This program was developed by educators and scientists working together to create meaningful and current curriculum for area high school students. The students have actually become a part of the effort to decode the human genome. They collect data and return them to the University of Washington so they can be used in the decoding process. The high school students recently contributed to decoding a gene responsible for inherited deafness.

To collect such data, the Human Genome unit is divided into three segments. The first segment, DNA synthesis, gets the students involved in building a piece of DNA. While doing this, students become familiar with laboratory equipment and procedures, and they gain an understanding of the components of DNA. The second segment involves the students in actually sequencing or decoding a piece of DNA. They obtain real data and report their findings back to the UW lab in both written and computer formats. The third segment explores bioethical decision making. For example, students are engaged in considering questions such: If we know that your genes indicate a propensity for a particular genetic disease, but we cannot treat you for its effects, what should we do with this information, and who should know what your genes indicate? Students are fascinated by these kinds of questions because they are challenging and profound and because society has not yet formulated responses to them.

Scientists have been involved in every part of the unit, both in its development and in classroom assistance and support to teachers. The equipment and reagents for these labs are funded through the Human Genome Project, which enables area school districts like our own to provide these experiences in the high school classroom.

Another source of current curriculum, equipment, and materials for area high school teachers is the Fred Hutchinson Science Research Center in Seattle. Teachers are required to apply to the Center's Science-Education Partnership (SEP) Program. If accepted, they are paired with a mentor scientist for approximately two weeks. The teachers assist and do research in one of several labs at the Hutchinson Center that participate in this effort, and they develop an aspect of curriculum to be used in their own science classrooms. These units are shared with other teachers in the program. Some of the more successful units have been put into kit form and travel throughout the Pacific Northwest, completely stocked with materials, equipment, reagents, and support information for the teachers. The first few kits were developed by educators and scientists working together, and the program has continued to grow from that beginning. In addition to the kits, SEP provides resource books, videos, expert advice, and visiting scientists. All of this support enables the classroom teacher to provide lab experiences to students that would not be available otherwise.

This past year I chose to include three of these work world-type labs in my honors biology classes. (One class is grade 9, the other is grade 10.) The labs I chose tied in well with the curriculum to be covered, addressed our Washington State Essential Learnings, and gave students work world applications for the knowledge they were gaining.

The first lab was from the High School Genome Project and worked with the sequencing of DNA, contributing as described above to a real piece of biological research. The second lab was a bacterial transformation lab from SEP. It involved incorporating a piece of DNA, a plasmid, into an existing bacteria and actually changing the genetic makeup of the bacteria. This change was observable in the color and growth pattern of the bacteria. The third lab was a bacterial identification lab that I developed in my previous career as a microbiologist that involved detecting and identifying different types of bacteria and determining which antibiotics should be used to treat a patient with a particular type of bacterial growth. All of these labs are being conducted in clinical or research laboratories, and all require the latest in biotechnology techniques and effective problem-solving skills. I believe these experiences are the closest to simulating work world laboratory science in the classroom possible.

I was curious about what the developers of these labs and my fellow biology teachers thought about the 100-minute period as a structure for supporting students as they conducted these labs that give them a realistic experience of doing science. In addition, I wanted feedback from students about how authentic they felt these lab experiences were and how they perceived the amount of time available to them to conduct the labs. I provided appropriate surveys to several curriculum developers and to teachers of the curriculum (see appendix C), and I surveyed 53 of my honors biology students (see appendixes A and B). Assisting scientists were also asked for their impressions of the 100-minute period and how realistic they felt these lab experiences were, compared with the laboratory workplace. I found the data from these inquiries to be very interesting, especially the student comments regarding the three labs.

The two assisting scientists who commented on these lab simulations had differing opinions about their authenticity. One scientist agreed with the statements that the lab he observed was "very authentic compared to work in his laboratory," and that the "lesson gives the student a good idea of how laboratories function." The other scientist indicated that parts of the lab seemed authentic, while other parts appeared contrived to fit it into a classroom situation. Both scientists, however, noted the benefit of having students involved in a hands-on lab experience.

The question of authenticity was summed up by one scientist:

> It is hard to design a lab that truly shows what research is like, but laboratories provide the tools to someday try out your own research and give a sense of what lab work is like. The best way to learn what research is like is to do it; independent research projects guided by teachers would be best. But I expect that teachers have too many things to do to take on this role, in addition to [buying] lab supplies that do cost money. I think you guys at Shorewood are doing a good job of trying creative approaches to making students think like scientists.

I found this to be valuable feedback. I appreciated the fact that the scientist understood some of the constraints on moving workplace lab experiences into the classroom, and I thought that his advice was well taken. It is always valuable for students to raise questions, develop a research strategy, carry out this strategy in the form of an experiment, and draw their own conclusions. Where possible, we do expand classroom activities to include these kinds of activities, although it is not usually as feasible in regular academic activities as it is with these work world simulations. With a vocational budget and more time allowed to develop student curriculum, I may be able to create more of these research-type experiences to be incorporated into a biotechnology class. As a department, we should try to do the same in our academic sciences classes.

As to whether the 100-minute period is viewed by these visiting scientists as being beneficial to a workplace simulation, both scientists felt that it depended on the lab experience in which the student was involved. One commented, "Whatever time is needed to go through a useful experiment and teamwork situation should be allocated; it teaches them [students] that project work sometimes needs more than mentality." Here the scientist is referring to the fact that lab work not only takes mental skills, but can require significant amounts of time devoted to more or less tedious tasks, as well.

Of course, it would be ideal to run lab classes by assigning whatever time students needed to complete each task, because that is the way labs function in the workplace. In the classroom this is not feasible, because we need to schedule science classes in conjunction with other subject areas. What is important to remember from the scientist's insight is that we need to instill in students the knowledge that scientific research takes time, and that it may not be completed in any set amount of time. Perhaps students could become responsible for scheduling their own lab workload to fit into our periods so they could develop a sense of control over their time and understand that experiments can go on for varying amounts of time, even for days or weeks. This kind of structure would provide further interwoven responsibility and independence for students and would simulate what occurs in the work world around breaks, appointments, holidays, and vacation times.

The three curriculum developers at SEP who interact daily with teachers using the SEP curriculum all believed that the labs were good at simulating work world experiences, although some labs were more effective at this than others. One explained, "The transformation lab is very work-oriented, while the electrophoresis lab is very much cookbook chemistry." All three agreed that the bacterial transformation lab that I conducted in my classes was one of the most effective at replicating a workplace experience. After developing these aspects of curriculum and working with the classroom teachers who used them, the three curriculum developers all agreed that 100-minute periods are better for these types of lab experiences. A curriculum developer explained, "In the real world you frequently have to just work till it's done. Plus, if you mess up, you have to start over and get it right. Those approaches are not feasible in the approximately 45 minutes of the standard class period (after checking roll, announcements, etc.). Learning to focus, stay on task, and plan your time are important work skills."

This comment by a SEP curriculum developer restated what some of the visiting scientists noted: a set, limited time such as a class period is difficult for lab work, because the worker must work until the job is done or else schedule the work to fit into the time allotted. It is easier for the teacher to recreate something like the work environment, and it certainly facilitates correcting errors if the students are given longer than 45 minutes per lab activity. The 100-minute period does enable students to function more independently and, thus, does provide a more realistic sense of what is expected in the workplace.

Finally, I queried my students' opinions regarding the work world simulation labs and the 100-minute periods in which we currently offer them (see appendixes A and B). These results were not necessarily what I expected, but I did gain some insight into the knowledge and impressions that students were taking from the experience of conducting these work world-type labs.

On the survey, students were asked to respond to a series of statements by marking the strength of their agreement (4 is high) or disagreement (1 is low). Statements that averaged a score of 3.5 from all students who completed the survey were considered as having received strong agreement. Students tended to strongly agree with the following statements:

- These lessons provided me with hands-on experiences.
- I found these lessons to be informative on how a laboratory is conducted.
- These lessons required participation on my part.
- It is important for students to participate in "real-world" educational experiences.

Students agreed (scores averaged from 2.6 to 3.4) with the need for hands-on labs and work world experiences in the classroom, according to this survey. However, the lowest score received by any of the statements came in response to the following one:

These lessons provided a work world simulation that increased my desire
to learn.

This response suggested to me that while most students did see the value of placing work world activities in the curriculum, some did not enjoy this type of activity. This may be due to the fact that not all students are taking biology because they
have a personal interest in this science. Biology is a required course at Shorewood,
and all students must take it to graduate. It also may be that even for some of those
students who do enjoy biology, the particular topic of biotechnology may not fas-
cinate them. Another factor may be that while ninth and tenth graders valued the
hands-on, active elements of these labs, they were less engaged by their work
world qualities because the world of work still seems distant to many of them.

Concerning the 100-minute periods, students agreed most strongly with the
statement: "These lessons require a longer class period (100 minutes) in order to
simulate a work world environment." This question received the most agreement of
all of the items on the survey. I also surveyed the 53 students about what they felt
would be the ideal length of a science class for the three labs that we were discussing. Ten percent of the students felt that less time would be sufficient, with the
lowest time span being a 60- to 80-minute period. None opted for the traditional
period of approximately 50 minutes. Twenty percent of the students felt we needed
a significantly longer period, with four students requesting all day or as long as
possible to run these labs. Seventy percent of the students felt 100 minutes was a
good time span for creating a work world experience for students. One student
commented: "The ideal time period to simulate a work world situation is 100 minutes, because I think we need breaks, and in the real work world, this could be a
lunch break. One hundred minutes is enough time to really get into the lab. It's a
realistic time period and it allows break time."

Some students also mentioned that if labs did last longer than 100-minutes, high
school students could lose interest or lose their capacity to retain knowledge. There
is likely some truth in these concerns. Even in the adult work world, breaks are
provided every one and a half to two hours. This would coincide nicely with a 100-
minute period and would simulate the different pieces of the workday (i.e., start to
morning break, morning break to lunch, lunch to afternoon break, and afternoon
break to day's end.) This insight gave me further cause to look at students scheduling their lab work within a 100-minute period, a length of time that, as noted by
both the scientists and SEP developers, encourages students to assume responsibility for conducting and completing their labs.

Conclusions

After examining the three work world components I currently use in my high
school science classroom to incorporate work world experiences, I have concluded

that the 100-minute period facilitates each of them and is strongly conducive to creating connections for students between their schooling and a relevant workplace experience.

In the experience component as enacted by job shadowing, the 100 minutes is particularly beneficial when the job shadow is short and can be conducted during the class period for which the student is doing the shadow (or that period and the additional 50 minutes for lunch). The greater benefit here, however, comes not from the 100-minute period, but from the three-period day. If the job shadow is an all-day venture, then the student misses at most three classes instead of the six in a traditional schedule. With greater ease in scheduling, and a larger push from schools for students to be involved in workplace experiences, more students will likely have the opportunity to be involved in educational experiences outside the classroom.

The second component, knowledge, brings scientists to the classroom to assist with labs and present information to students. While my very small sample of visiting scientists did not make a case for the value of block periods in relation to their participation, it seems evident to me that 100-minute periods are likely to encourage scientists to visit high school classrooms for longer periods of time if their travel time and distance is the same for block periods as it would be for short periods. For each trip back and forth from their workplace to my school, scientists are likely to give us twice as much of their time in our classrooms.

The most revealing information for me came from the third component, in which I evaluated the classroom activities that simulate workplace experiences and the impact of 100-minute periods on such activities. Students, curriculum developers, and scientists all found that work world labs simulated work experiences. They gave the students a sense of being involved in a work world activity and engaged them in the exploration of new and relevant topics in science.

One 100-minute periods tend to accentuate the workplace qualities of these labs. Block periods give students time to understand the material, learn equipment use, complete an experiment in a more realistic, work world context, and develop the skills to complete these labs. So block periods are seen by students and teachers as far preferable to shorter periods, with 90 percent of the students needing 100 minutes or longer to complete one of these labs satisfactorily.

Finally, as was pointed out by teachers, students, and visiting scientists, perhaps the key issue in relation to 100-minute periods and high school science education centers is how the teacher chooses to structure the use of this time in relation to the curriculum. What this study reinforced for me was my commitment to encouraging my students to become more responsible for figuring out and scheduling their own workloads and use of time during the lab activities, much as one would be required to do in the workplace. With 100 minutes, I also know that if a student does make an error or needs extra time, we will often be able to accommodate this circumstance.

As for my new vocational biotechnology class, the curriculum and learning outcomes are not mandated as they are in the regular biology class, so I will have more freedom to explore various aspects of these work world components. Following the recommendations of the visiting scientists and the SEP personnel, I will provide students with more time to conduct independent research. This should include asking questions, designing labs, coordinating and running the labs, collecting data, and analyzing the data. I can structure the 100-minute period to represent a part of a workday (i.e., afternoon break until the end of the day), and students will need to work out their own schedules to complete a longer-term project over several days or even weeks. My hope is that such a structure will simulate the work world and deepen students' engagement in learning because they will develop increased interest in and ownership of their research.

Appendix A

Evaluation for High School Students with the Average Scores of the 53 Students Surveyed

As "work world" learning experiences, how would you rate the lessons you participated in that involved labs supplied by the various research centers (i.e., DNA Sequencing, Bacterial Identification and Transformation labs)?

The number 1 indicates that you strongly disagree, 2 that you disagree, 3 that you agree with the statement, and 4 that you strongly agree with the statement.

					Average
1. These lessons modeled an experience likely to be encountered in the work world.	1	2	3	4	2.9
2. These lessons provided me with a hands-on work experience.	1	2	3	4	3.5
3. I found these lessons to be informative as to how work in a laboratory is conducted.	1	2	3	4	3.5
4. This project gave me a feeling of responsibility.	1	2	3	4	2.8
5. These lessons provided a working world simulation that increased my desire to learn.	1	2	3	4	2.6
6. I found these lessons to be very realistic in terms of a workplace situation.	1	2	3	4	2.8
7. The DNA lesson was rewarding in terms of my ability to contribute data to an actual experiment.	1	2	3	4	3.2
8. These lessons provided me with useful information I can use in the future.	1	2	3	4	2.7
9. I can apply this information to other areas and other working situations.	1	2	3	4	2.7
10. I found this project helpful in understanding the laboratory work world.	1	2	3	4	3.2
11. I consider this to be a valuable experience for a high school student.	1	2	3	4	3.3
12. These lessons required participation on my part.	1	2	3	4	3.5
13. I found these lessons to be educationally motivating.	1	2	3	4	2.8
14. I found these lessons to be educationally rewarding.	1	2	3	4	2.9
15. I learned a great deal about the laboratory work world from these lessons.	1	2	3	4	3.0
16. These lessons require a longer class period (100 minutes) to simulate a work world environment.	1	2	3	4	3.6

Average

17. It is important for students to participate in
    "real-world" educational experiences.   1   2   3   4   3.5

18. It is important for students to have scientists assist
    with and answer questions during these lessons.   1   2   3   4   3.2

Please give a brief answer to each question below.

Reflecting on your experience in this class concerning the DNA sequencing, transformation lab, and bacterial identification lab, what do you think would be the ideal length of time for a class session to simulate a work world situation involving these lessons? Why?

Do you feel longer science class periods are necessary to incorporate real world learning in the science curriculum? Why or why not?

Appendix B

Ideal Length of the Classroom Period Involving Work World Simulated Labs

(Data collected from written response on student survey, appendix A)

<100-minute periods	*100-minute periods*	*>100-minute periods*
5 students	36 students	10 students
5/53 = 10 percent	36/53 = 70 percent	10/53 students = 20 percent

Comments:

60–80 minutes

75 minutes

95 minutes

85 minutes

80–90 minutes

Comments:

3 hours

6–8 hours

all day

all day

the longer the better

all day

greater than 100 minutes

2–3 hours each day

120 minutes

as long as possible

Appendix C

Evaluation for Science Program Developers with the Average Scores Recorded

I am currently evaluating our 100-minute periods and attempting to determine if they help us to provide a greater sense of a real "work world" situation than do other length classroom periods. I feel that the labs we are using provided by the SEP program (or by the University of Washington Molecular Biotechnology Program) are some of the best at providing current materials and a sense of what occurs in actual work world lab settings. Since you communicate with the many teachers who routinely check labs out from your facility and you have a good impression of what these instructors are feeling, could you please answer the following questions concerning the Gel Electrophoresis and Transformation labs?

The number 1 indicates that you strongly disagree, 2 indicates that you disagree, 3 that you agree with the statement, and 4 that you strongly agree with the statement.

					Average Score
1. These lessons modeled an experience likely to be encountered in the work world.	1	2	3	4	4
2. These lessons provide students with a hands-on work experience.	1	2	3	4	4
3. These lessons are informative as to how work in a laboratory is conducted.	1	2	3	4	3.7
4. These lessons give students a feeling of responsibility.	1	2	3	4	3.7
5. These lessons provide a work world simulation that increases a students' desire to learn.	1	2	3	4	3.7
6. I found these lessons to be very realistic in terms of a workplace situation.	1	2	3	4	3.3
7. The transformation lesson is authentic in terms of actually changing the DNA makeup of a living organism and participating in a current experiment.	1	2	3	4	4
8. These lessons provide students with useful information they can use in the future.	1	2	3	4	3.7
9. Students can apply this information to other areas and other working situations.	1	2	3	4	3.7
10. I consider this project to be helpful in understanding the laboratory work world.	1	2	3	4	4
11. I consider this to be a valuable experience for a high school student.	1	2	3	4	4

						Average Score
12.	These lessons required participation on the students' part.	1	2	3	4	4
13.	These lessons are educationally motivating.	1	2	3	4	4
14.	These lessons are educationally rewarding.	1	2	3	4	3.7
15.	Students learn a great deal about the laboratory work world from these lessons.	1	2	3	4	3.7
16.	These lessons require a longer class period (100 minutes) to simulate a work world environment.	1	2	3	4	3.5
17.	It is important for students to participate in "real-world" educational experiences.	1	2	3	4	4
18.	It is important for students to have scientists assist with and answer questions during these lessons.	1	2	3	4	3.3

Please give brief answers to the each question below.

1. Reflecting on your experience and communication with science teachers, what do you think is the ideal length of time for a science class session to provide the optimal experience for science students involved with these lessons? Why?
2. Do you feel longer class periods provide a better example of a real "work world" situation? Why or why not?

Appendix D

Evaluation for Guest Scientists in the Classroom

I am currently evaluating the length of a high school science class period and its effect on providing "work world" or authentic lab experiences for students. You recently helped out in a classroom that has 100-minute periods. I would like to have your impression, from a scientist's point of view, about whether 100-minute periods help to provide a "work world" experience for students that seems to simulate the workplace. Please answer the following six questions concerning your experience in the classroom.

1. Which portion of the DNA Sequencing Lab did you assist on?
   A. Day 1—Setting up the samples to be tested
   B. Day 2—Injecting and running the gels
   C. Day 3—Preparing and washing the membranes.

2. The lesson I observed was authentic compared to an actual laboratory.
   A. Strongly Disagree
   B. Disagree
   C. Agree
   D. Strongly Agree

3. The lesson gives the students a good idea of how laboratories function.
   A. Strongly disagree
   B. Disagree
   C. Agree
   D. Strongly Agree

4. I think the ideal time for a high school science class incorporating such labs should be:
   A. less then or equal to 55 minutes.
   B. approximately 75–80 minutes.
   C. approximately 95–105 minutes.
   D. more then 105 minutes.
   E. The time is irrelevant.

5. I think the most valuable part of this lesson for students that would help them to appreciate the work world is:
   A. information provided by the teacher.
   B. hands-on experience in the lab.
   C. cooperative group work required for this lab.
   D. the chance to question and work with scientists.
   E. other (explain).

6. The time interval for a class session that makes it the easiest for me to participate is:
   A. 55 min.
   B. approx. 80 min.
   C. approx. 100 min.
   D. >100 min.
   E. doesn't matter

6

Motivating the Alternative
Learner in 100-Minute Periods

Amy Chertock and Jennifer Evans
Shorewood High School

> Amy Chertock, a social studies teacher, and Jennifer Evans, an English
> teacher, both teach in the alternative education program at Shorewood
> High School that serves students who are at risk. They wanted to study
> how they could better use the 100-minute block period to increase the
> motivation of their students for constructive participation and learning.
> Through careful analysis of their own teaching and their students' actions
> and reflections, they identified five strategies that promoted greater stu-
> dent engagement and success in school.

Introduction and Program Description

For our alternative education classroom, we have created a school-within-a-school
structure where heavy emphasis is placed on the mentoring relationship between
teacher and student, student-centered instruction, and applied learning with authentic assessment. Students are assigned to classes depending on their skills or needs
rather than grade level. We have 100-minute periods four days each week with an
ABC structure (described in chapter 1), and we wanted to explore how best to maximize the benefits of the block period with our at-risk population.

When we reflected on how to manage our class time most effectively, we concluded that we could not separate the teacher's best use of the 100-minute block
from our students' general lack of motivation to learn. The relationship between
these two elements is what led us to our research question: How can we best use
the 100-minute period to increase student motivation in our alternative classrooms?

An insight that intrigued both of us was the correlation between the personalized
teaching and learning that takes place in an alternative education program and the personalized motivation techniques used by effective athletic coaches. Both of us coach
high school sports: Amy, cross country and the distance events on the track and field
team, and Jennifer, basketball and the throwing events on the track and field team. De-

spite the considerable differences in setting and students between athletics and the alternative education program (athletics are voluntary, for example; school usually is not), we both noticed that we were applying our coaching skills in the classroom.

We also hoped to use this research as an opportunity to examine what the teacher of at-risk students can learn from the best motivational practices of coaching. There are many parallels between coaching and teaching alternative education, including multiage grouping of students, personalized relationships over multiple years, individualized coaching and instruction, and acknowledgment that there are many ways for an individual to accomplish a goal.

Description of the Independent Learning Center (ILC)

Shorewood's alternative education program, the Independent Learning Center (ILC), is an on-site program that is integrated functionally with the rest of the school. It has an academic, achievement-oriented focus. The program adheres to the same discipline and attendance policies as the entire school. Many kinds of alternative schools exist, both locally and nationwide. Ours can be described as a "Beef 'Em Up and Send 'Em Back" program. Our ultimate goal is to help students reconnect with school, value their education as a tool that will help them gain control over their lives and futures, and develop their learning skills so they can meet the standards successfully in a regular class. Students do not always return to the regular classroom after a stint in the ILC, but it is certainly a positive goal for many students. This focus is driven in part by our structure as a relatively small department within a fairly large, academically focused high school.

ILC Classes

The ILC offers a variety of learning structures. Students can take one or more classes in the ILC during the school day. These classes are offered first through sixth period and include: English, Speech, U.S. History, Contemporary Problems/Current Events, Mastery Math, Health, and Art. These classes are smaller than the school's average, often 10–15 students, and they are very interactive, with both individual and whole-group instruction. Participation and regular attendance are critical to each student's success. Classes tend to develop their own personalities very quickly, and ILC teachers work hard to create a positive dynamic and sense of belonging and community within each class group.

This action research was conducted in ILC classes.

(ILC students at Shorewood can also earn independent, contract-based credits, with two formats available. In one format a student is scheduled into a regular 100-minute class period where attendance is required. The student must complete a preestablished set of requirements to gain the credit. There may be 1 to 10 or 12 students in the classroom at a time, each working on her/his own assignments. In this format students have at least one staff member available to assist them at all times. The other option involves students completing contract classes on their own time, outside school hours and generally off-campus. When students contract for such credits, they must meet with an ILC teacher for at least one hour each week.)

Types of Students Who Are in the ILC

It is difficult to describe the typical ILC student, because the reasons for students' lack of success in a regular classroom can be as widely disparate as the students themselves. Nonetheless students who enter the ILC generally embody a combination of several or more of the following descriptors:

- They are returning to school after having dropped out.
- They are on the verge of dropping out and/or are involved in the truancy courts.
- They have failed multiple courses.
- They are unproductive in their classes in terms of participation and class-work/homework.
- They express a strong feeling of "not fitting in."
- They are ADD-ADHD.
- They have chronic physical and/or mental health conditions.
- They have no particular learning disability but are behind grade level in their reading and writing skills.
- They use or abuse drugs and/or have a history of drug use.
- They are court-involved.

A variety of factors lead students to be placed or to place themselves in smaller, more personalized programs such as the ILC. We have found that the common thread among our ILC students at Shorewood is low academic motivation. On an encouraging note, though, this does not necessarily mean that these students are unmotivated workers or learners in all contexts. Rather, for these students, the world of the classroom could not be any further removed or disconnected from their perception of "the real world." The absolute apathy among these teens toward the academic skills and knowledge that schools are accountable for teaching rarely corresponds with an apathy toward work and learning in "the real world." This provides us with the challenge as teachers of predominantly at-risk students to help our students make connections between what they want to learn and do outside of school and what school can offer them.

What Distinguishes the ILC from the Regular Program at Shorewood?

How does the educational experience of students differ if they take classes in the ILC? There are three structural program differences that have a tremendous impact: first, class sizes are quite small in the ILC; second, students have the same teachers for more than one period and for more than one year; and third, there are students of different grade levels in each class.

These structural features enable us to provide students with a number of benefits. For example, each student receives much more support and assistance in completing work. Teachers are able to individualize their instruction more readily, making accommodations for students' learning strengths, weaknesses, and interests. Curriculum is very flexible and student-centered in the ILC. Students are encouraged to take responsibility for their own learning and are invited to bring their experiences and interests to the classroom. Curriculum is covered at a slower pace and with less range than in the traditional classroom, but the target skills are the same, and content is covered in a great deal of depth. There is a concerted effort to emphasize work and life skills across the curriculum, sometimes in lieu of the more academic, college-prep skills. Teaching toward multiple intelligences is also heavily emphasized in the ILC classes, with an effort to incorporate as many kinesthetic tasks as possible to teach skills and content.

The Research Question and Research Process

When we began our research, we were very excited about analyzing a number of the variables that we consider in our day-to-day teaching. The main theme to which we returned continually in our analysis was low motivation of our students. We understand that low motivation is generally a manifestation of other critical conditions in a student's life that we can rarely do anything about. Nonetheless, we experience the impact of students' low motivation in our classrooms daily. We found ourselves reflecting on lessons that went well ("Wow! The kids were so motivated today—I could feel the learning and energy in the air!") and those that went poorly ("Geez, this might have been a neat lesson, but the kids were so unmotivated. They never gave it a try!"). We realized that a closer examination of what we were doing differently on the "motivated" days versus the "unmotivated" might reveal a set of best practices we could then apply to all of our planning and teaching. From this thinking, we developed our primary research question:

> How can we best use the 100-minute block period to increase student motivation in our alternative classrooms?

Motivation means different things to different people. For us, our students were motivated when they were engaged in the learning activity, had a positive attitude while completing it, and felt a need to learn more. We wanted the students to find a connection between the lessons being taught and their own lives as they perceived them. In our daily reflections we noted that many of the behaviors we saw in our students that were not conducive to learning occurred when there was no such connection.

We developed two data collection tools to assist us in this examination. We used Reflection Journal sheets (see appendix A) after each lesson during a seven-week period to record our choices in planning our lessons, our observations of student motivation, and our evolving theories about what practices worked best. We also developed a Student Motivation Inventory (see appendix B) that the students filled out toward the end of a large unit of study. This survey gave students a chance to reflect on their own work and motivation and to indicate which actions of ours, if any, affected their motivation.

Data Collection and Results

In our research we tried many teaching and motivational strategies with varied English curriculum to accomplish the goal of using the 100-minute block period to increase students' motivation. Jennifer was working with a career unit, while Amy was simultaneously trying to find ways to motivate students to participate in a unit about a novel.

Reflection Journals

We engaged in intensive, structured self-reflection after each lesson in these units. What emerged for both of us was a number of specific strategies that we used as teachers that directly affected our students' motivation to carry out learning activities. As we reflected on these strategies, we found that five emerged as most effective in relation to our objective:

1. providing clear and explicit written directions for students (especially when they are working in a new setting, such as the library or career center)
2. emphasizing and developing students' pride in their program
3. role-playing behavior expectations repeatedly with students
4. listening to and responding to student concerns
5. connecting lessons and units to what students perceived as "the real world" of their lives

Following are specific examples of how we used these strategies and how they affected our students' motivation.

Jennifer explains: The career unit I was completing involved a research component, a writing component, and a speech component. The students were to research a career of their choice and report their findings to the class about how to achieve success in that particular career. We completed our research in the school's career lab and went on two field trips: to a local business and to a successful training program at a local community college. These trips were intended to inform my students about the many job options found in one established business and the kind of training required to become qualified for various positions.

One challenge within the alternative classroom is that any change in structure—in this case, the location—can destroy class order and cohesion. One effective response to this challenge is to give specific tasks to each student to accomplish in the new setting. The tasks should be written down in the form of a list, because specification of task steps is essential. Students need to discuss in class what their goals are for the visit. They need to develop a list of questions to ask and bring a copy of the list of tasks and questions with them on the visit.

When we went on our first trip to the career center, I had not equipped students with a written copy of tasks and questions. We had discussed these in class, but my verbal advice of what to do and where to find information was not adequate for students' needs. Many students wandered around aimlessly and were bored or distracted. On reflection, I realized that the students' failure to perform was a result of their lack of clarity about what to do next and their lack of any reference for the progress they were making. These conditions adversely affected their motivation and led to many behavioral problems. These problems changed my role from providing facilitation and assistance to enforcing discipline.

For our next field trip I typed up a list of questions and distributed them and our discussion notes as a handout on the day of the trip. It was important that students had the list so they could refer to it and take notes about the responses they received. That field trip out of school and the next one were both very successful because of several factors. First, students had clear, written directions about what they needed to accomplish. Second, teachers need to foster pride within students for the program in which they are involved. If the teacher is not respectful of and confident in the students' abilities, the students will not feel the desire to act respectfully. Also, the students truly need to take ownership of the lesson and mold it to suit their needs. Before venturing out of the classroom we discussed appropriate behavior and role-played what it would look like to someone outside the program if we behaved improperly. That opportunity for student reflection was an important element of the field trip's success. It displayed both poor and appropriate behavior in a nonaccusatory way. Humor can be a very powerful tool. By showing students some poor choices in a comical manner, I managed to make it seem ridiculous to act inappropriately and successfully supported good behavior.

We visited a car dealership as our established business. Girls were the minority in the class I took, and they felt that I was catering to the boys' stereotypical love of cars. I explained to them that the auto industry, though male-dominated, appeals to both genders. Almost everyone in his/her lifetime will own a car. I encouraged the female students to generate questions that satisfied their own needs about purchasing a car. I also encouraged them to ask questions pertaining to the jobs in the dealership, rather than the mechanical workings of a car. We discussed how each job position is analogous to a different customer-oriented business. By taking the time to discuss my female students' needs, I significantly increased their willingness to learn. Teachers need to treat their students with respect. They need to listen to their likes and dislikes. If we do not listen to what the students are saying and address the issues they raise, we will lose their respect, and they will be less willing to learn in our classrooms. Students' success goes hand-in-hand with their need and motivation to learn.

When it comes to reading, writing, and communication, the alternative learner typically does not see the need to practice these skills. During our visits I required the students to ask the employees whom they interviewed which high school classes they found most beneficial. One hundred percent of those who were asked about the importance of English class to their job responded that communication skills were an area the workers were constantly trying to improve. This response had a huge impact on the students when they found out how people could be ridiculed by their colleagues for poor grammar or spelling in an office memo or inadequate expression in a meeting. This work setting also gave me new ideas for language-based classroom assignments that could be published in the classroom or school. Our first assignment was to write thank-you letters to the individuals at the different establishments who took the time to show us around. This was a very successful lesson.

Another assignment the students were asked to complete was to reflect on what kinds of activities they already like to perform and how those could best fit with a particular job they observed. The students really enjoyed this writing assignment because it was based solely on their interests and how those interests applied to the real world. Many had never thought that a job might also be something they liked to do. This realization created a very positive atmosphere within the classroom and helped some students begin to look toward their post-high school future in a new way.

Amy explains: During this same time period, I was working with an English class of 14 students. The main activity going on was a novel unit; our goal was to read John Steinbeck's *Cannery Row*. Common complaints from the students about reading are that they hated reading, there are no good books, and "reading's not for me; I'll NEVER like it." This attitude gave me some pause, but I felt that the benefits of our reading a novel together as a tool for learning key English concepts would outweigh the struggle to overcome the students' resistance.

I used a variety of approaches and techniques during this unit to meet my objectives for the students, and some were more effective than others. The first of the five strategies that we felt led to the highest levels of motivation with our students was providing clear and explicit written directions before having students start a new task. For me, this meant having each day's plans written on the board in great detail and having additional printed handouts available with directions for any activities that were not a part of our daily routine. This may seem like common sense for all teachers, but I can't overemphasize the importance for at-risk learners in particular of having information available in a variety of ways to guide them through lessons. I also felt that writing the different stages of the lesson on the board in different-colored ink, and having the printed handouts on different-colored paper, was very helpful when referring students back to the plan for the day.

On the rushed days when I didn't get the plan for the day written in enough step-by-step detail, I definitely noticed much lower productivity and motivation. By the time we were midway through the class period and I was trying to give oral directions one-on-one, I found that there was much less willingness on the part of students to put effort into the assignment, and that they were more likely to try to engage in a back-and-forth over what was really required. For example, "You didn't SAY that this essay needs to have more than one sentence!" So, the availability of crystal clear instructions for students in all but the most routine parts of a lesson is one key to increasing motivation, particularly with at-risk students. They feel secure when they understand your expectations fully, and they are much more willing to put energy and quality into their work.

Another activity I used to increase student motivation was to build pride and a sense of community in the ILC program. There is always a risk in taking non- or low-achieving students out of a mainstream class and putting them together, but when that class or program can be seen by kids as a privilege and a choice, it can have a very positive effect on their learning. In terms of motivating students to want to read *Cannery Row*, I encouraged them to look at some of the themes of the novel, such as community, individuality, and respect, and to compare them with the themes of our program. I made sure that students knew that theirs was the only class I was aware of that studied this particular book, making it a special experience for us. I referred often to "what it means to study in the ILC . . ." to give the program an identity and give students a sense of belonging to a group. This is something a teacher can do with every class, even if he or she is not teaching in a special program, and it ties in very clearly with techniques used by coaches to motivate and drive athletes.

Another activity I observed to be very effective during this unit was role-playing both the positive and the negative behaviors that I was seeing in students as we read the novel. This was something I did in a fairly lighthearted way to demonstrate what active listening does and does not look like. After one frustrating lesson during which students were either comatose or aggressively attempting to take each other off-task, I decided to prepare the students for the next discussion with an admittedly overly dramatized sample of what I'd seen the day before. First I simply imitated some of the disruptive behaviors while one student attempted to summarize the events of the chapters we'd read the day before. I asked students how it felt to them when they were trying to say something they felt was important and no one was listening. Then I had students work in pairs for two minutes, with one person talking the whole time and the other listening. We discussed what nonverbal actions the listener can take to participate in the discussion, and how it felt to the speaker to have the listener acting in those ways. The students enjoyed doing the role-plays and saw the connection between role-playing and real behavior in class. Just as a coach needs to isolate athletic skills and provide time and structure for athletes to practice them, teachers need to do exactly the same with academic skills. In this case, my students needed to practice the listening skills that I thought they were capable of.

One key strategy the 100-minute period facilitates is giving students an authentic voice in planning the curriculum and class instruction. This must be done carefully; you do not want to give students the impression that they have veto power over everything, but no responsibility for suggesting activities. It is essential to listen carefully and respond to students' opinions and concerns about class activities; it is not essential, however, always to modify or cancel those activities about which students have concerns. In fact, students don't expect that. The atmosphere of respect and trust that grows from giving full attention to student concerns is essential to have students begin to see themselves as responsible for their own learning, which becomes motivating in itself.

One of my grave concerns as I started the novel unit with my English class was the fact that attendance is so inconsistent in the ILC. This is an elemental and very frustrating factor in teaching classes of at-risk students; students don't come every day. I decided to broach this topic with students on the first day of the unit. I explained my objectives for teaching this book, what I hoped the students would gain from the experience, and the types of activities we would be doing to supplement the reading over the next six weeks or so. Then I outlined some of the behaviors I really loved about this class of students and those I found frustrating, and how the latter set of behaviors could negatively affect studying the book. I asked the students what they thought of my concerns, and what suggestions they had for how to deal with them, keeping our objectives in mind.

The students responded wonderfully. They talked as a whole group among themselves, moderating their own discussion, and they agreed on a plan for students to be responsible for making up chapters independently when they were absent. They advised me to map out a schedule of which chapters would be read each day and stick to it. Some acknowledged that they had never read a whole book before, and they were starting to get excited about the prospect. One girl declared she would not be absent one day until we finished the book—and she kept her word! There was a wonderful dynamic in the class that day, and I had never felt such buy-in about a project or long-term task from an alternative education class before. The energy waxed and waned a bit during the following weeks, but no one ever questioned why we were reading the book or how much work we needed to get done on a particular day. In reflecting back, I realize that I never gave students the option of getting out of the work to be done. I just gave them the task of figuring out the best way to get it done, and they rose to the challenge.

The final high-priority need when planning instructional activities is to incorporate a connection between the world our students experience beyond school and the material studied in class. In the case of teaching *Cannery Row*, I was able to integrate a number of current events, particularly related to the economy and homelessness in Seattle. Students were engaged in reading newspaper articles. They also practiced their cause-and-effect and compare-contrast skills through exploring the causes of homelessness in this city and comparing them to the community of transients who populated *Cannery Row*. We also used the real world of Shorewood High School as a realm for deep character analysis by writing about what kind of students the different characters would be if they attended Shorewood, using examples from the text to back up our assertions about each character. These activities helped students relate the book to their lives and increased their motivation to read it. There were impromptu discussions about which characters were cooler, and the students would pause independently in the middle of important events in the story to predict how the characters might respond and, even better, to say how they would have reacted in the same circumstances. In sum, any and all efforts on the part of the teacher to help students build connections between what they learn in school and what they experience in "their real world" pays off greatly in increasing student motivation.

Student Surveys

The one consistent theme that we discovered in our students' comments on the Student Motivation Inventory was the powerful impact of clear and immediate connections between what we were doing in class and our students' perceptions of their "real lives" outside of school. Without this kind of immediate relationship, few of our students could recognize the application of particular school lessons to the larger picture of their lives. When our students did perceive these connections, they were much more likely to be motivated to learn in our classrooms, behave appropriately, and make an effort to learn.

We also asked students if receiving individual attention affected their level of motivation. As coaches we see direct, personal contact with an athlete as a vital motivational tool. This positive contact is so important to self-esteem and future success. The students responded that for the most part having interaction with the teacher helped them focus and motivated them to want to work harder on the activity. Providing one-to-one interaction between teacher and student and giving positive attention to students for good work are critical to enhancing student motivation.

Conclusion

What are the most effective ways to use the 100-minute block period to increase student motivation in our alternative classrooms? We identified five important strategies that we came to use regularly with increasing success:

- providing clear instructions
- developing students' pride in their program
- identifying explicit student behavior expectations
- listening to student concerns
- connecting lessons and units to what students perceived as "the real world" of their lives

We believe that the 100-minute block period provides greater opportunity to implement these strategies with our students because the larger blocks of time encourage us as teachers to integrate most or all of these strategies in significant ways into every class period. With 100 minutes we have time to pay attention to our students more intensively and focus on the curriculum. This individual attention is essential in our alternative classrooms because, as our students told us, personal attention from the teacher increases their motivation to learn.

Our research also led us to the following conclusions:

- Both our classroom observations and our students' comments supported our hypothesis that making a connection between the lesson and our students' perceptions of their lives outside of school is powerfully motivating for the students. With the 100-minute period, students have more time to reflect on how the content and skills they are learning are related to their lives. The teacher has greater opportunity to encourage students one-on-one to think about each lesson's content within the context of their lives.
- Our reflections confirmed for us that coaching and teaching are more directly related than we had assumed initially. A good coach is someone who is an effective teacher, an excellent motivator, and a positive role model. A good teacher can be quite similar. The best teachers and coaches are those who develop each student's/athlete's skills and show each student/athlete how to set and reach new goals.
- We learned through our reflections that the 100-minute period behooves us to look more closely at all of the teaching/learning activities we plan: their purpose, their sequence, and their relationship with each other. For a 100-minute period to work for students, the parts need to be fit together effectively by the teacher.
- Finally, our reflections informed us that the 100-minute period accelerates the process of learning about our students' individual needs and capabilities, because we spend more time together during each class meeting. By reducing the administrative time in our week, we can increase the time spent in interacting with our students. The ultimate, and ultimately rewarding, result of this is freeing up more time and energy to motivate students and, even more important, to help them see the ways and reasons to motivate themselves.

Appendix A

Reflection Journal

Date:

Lesson Plan & Learning Goals:

Breakdown of Time Line:

Individual Student Behavior:

How did I change the plan according to student behavior, or how would I change the lesson in the future?

Appendix B

Student Motivation Inventory

Student Name: _____

Intensity and Direction to Reach Goal:

1. What is the goal of this exercise?

2. Can you apply this goal to "real life"?

3. How?

4. How much effort are you putting forth to achieve this goal? (circle one)
    0 = none   1 = very little   2 = enough to get by   3 = satisfies requirement
    4 = above and beyond

5. Explain why you evaluated your effort this way.

6. How many times has the teacher helped you individually?

7. Did you ask for help, or what were you doing when I volunteered my help?

8. After I helped you, how did your feelings change toward the exercise?

Student Comments:

My Comments:

7

Cross-Age Teaching in Block Periods: High School Students Teaching Elementary Students

Tracy Stoops
Shorewood High School

Tracy Stoops wanted to investigate the experience of her mostly senior Marine Biology students while they tutored elementary students about whales, an academic/service learning project made possible by 100-minute block periods. She hypothesized that they would benefit from this experience because (1) one of the best ways to learn is to teach, and (2) their engagement with the children would heighten their sense of responsibility for their own learning.

Her data indicate that her students learned a great deal about whales, community involvement, and interacting with younger students. The data also show the ways she could structure this project so that the high school students would gain more content learning from its activities.

Introduction

The two schools involved in this study, Shorewood High School (described in chapter 1) and one of its feeder schools, Parkwood Elementary School, are both in the Shoreline School District. Parkwood Elementary, with 300 students, is one of the more diverse elementary schools in the district, both ethnically and socio-economically.

The focus of this study was a project in which high school students in a Marine Biology course at Shorewood taught a unit about whales to elementary students at Parkwood. Two different circumstances made this a perfect time to begin such an effort. First, beginning this past year, Shorewood and Parkwood had both become partners in the ATLAS (Authentic Teaching Learning and Assessment) Project, along with all of the other schools in the "west corridor" of the district. One of the ATLAS goals is to encourage communication and curricular alignment among K–12 sending and receiving schools. This project supports that effort. Second,

Shorewood has adopted a block period schedule, and for the past three years we have had an ABC schedule: four days of three 100-minute periods ("A" days and "B" days) and one day of 50-minute periods ("C" days). This schedule gave the high school students the opportunity to travel to the elementary school twice a week, teach a lesson, and return in time for their next class, which was not possible with the traditional school schedule.

The Marine Biology class at Shorewood consisted of 31 students: 27 seniors and 4 juniors. Twenty-six of the students had been successful in science previously, earning a B or better in Biology. They were able to provide their own transportation between the schools.

The Parkwood teachers who volunteered to participate, Cathi Wrolstad and Chuck Orser, each taught a multiage grade 1–2 class of 24 students. Flexibility was built into Parkwood's schedule, which allowed the times of the science unit to work out for both schools involved.

The topic we covered, whales, was chosen because of its place in the Marine Biology curriculum, children's interest in it, and the availability of curricular materials. The materials provided by the high school for the elementary student labs were taken from a curriculum developed by the Pacific Science Center in Seattle, which provided inquiry-based learning at the K–3 level.

It was deemed self-evident that it would be beneficial for the elementary students to be tutored by a high school student "teacher" at a ratio of three elementary students to one high school student, allowing for personal attention for each child from the "teacher." My hypothesis was that my Marine Biology students would also gain from this experience because (1) one of the best ways to learn is to teach, and (2) their engagement with the children would heighten their sense of responsibility for their own learning. This study explores the value of the teaching experience for high school students, an experience made possible by our block period structure.

Research Questions

- Is teaching elementary students a valuable experience for high school students?
- Does their teaching of elementary students promote high school students' knowledge and understanding of relevant curriculum?
- What are the benefits and costs of such a cross-age teaching endeavor?

Description of Process

To begin this project, my students needed to define what they understood a *valuable educational experience* to be. After discussing my research questions with my colleagues, I settled on having the students brainstorm ideas about what constituted a *valuable learning experience*. Each student shared one experience she/he considered to be a stellar moment in learning, one that stood out as a major achievement. I jotted the students' contributions onto the overhead (appendix A). We then examined these experiences and discussed what characterized them as valuable (appendix A). The descriptive words generated through this process were then incorporated into a set of three questionnaires (appendixes D, E, and F) that we used as an evaluation tool at the end of the project.

Note that only 6 of the 25 experiences that students identified as *educationally valuable* dealt directly with school-related activities or occurred in a classroom setting. Most students used a criterion for value that focused on whether what they had learned was useful to them in their own personal lives and whether they would continue to use the information and/or skills they had gained through the experience. In other words, the students were not as concerned with school-focused issues as they were with the relevance of the information and/or skills. Keep in mind that these were mostly seniors getting ready to graduate. They were actively seeking skills and knowledge that were useful beyond the high school setting, and they may have entered this discussion in a different frame of mind from a younger group of students whose goals are centered around their own completion of high school.

The project itself consisted of four parts: an introductory activity, preparation for the teaching, the actual teaching of the lessons, and several different forms of project evaluation.

Introductory Activity

There is an IMAX theater located in downtown Seattle at the Pacific Science Center, which, coincidentally, was showing the movie, *Whales*. We decided to introduce this project by beginning to develop relationships between the Parkwood students and the Shorewood students through their attending a showing of this movie together. While we were lined up to enter the theater, students mingled and introductions were made. This was an entertaining time for me as an educator. Watching the younger students admiring the high school students, and the high school students enjoying the elementary students' enthusiasm for the field trip and their variety of questions ("Wow! How did you get so tall!" or "So, Sara, where do baby whales come from?") led me to believe this would be a memorable experience for all. The downside was that we did not have a long enough opportunity for sharing among these students, nor was the atmosphere conducive to communicating at length. All of the students saw the movie, which provided information appropriate for all grade levels. The biggest benefit was simply creating a common experience for all involved in the project to share.

Preparation for Teaching

Substantial organizing was needed to prepare the high school students to teach the lessons, which explored whales' types, sizes, and features; special environmental adaptations of whales; and sonar location. The project included four lessons for the elementary students, each of which required about 50 minutes. All of the 31 high school students in my Marine Biology class were taught each of the elementary lessons in a large-group class, with two lessons completed in each 100-minute period. In addition they had one 50-minute class to practice teaching their lessons to each other. The preparation time prior to teaching took exactly one week.

The lessons were fairly straightforward, inquiry-based, and largely in kit form. These materials had been tested in numerous classrooms and workshops before we used them. I was concerned at first that the concepts would be mostly review for my high school students, but there was an extensive amount of information for the teacher in the curriculum kit that supplemented the simple lessons and offered my students challenging new insights and information about whales.

The catch came when I expected my students to read and comprehend this material. The students did less reading about and researching of their topics than I had expected. This result decreased the amount of academic challenge my students experienced and left them less prepared to teach the lessons in an in-depth manner than I had expected. In retrospect I realize that I needed to give my students more structure and greater accountability as they researched the background information for their lessons.

The two 100-minute periods seemed to provide adequate time to cover these four simple lessons. Most students seemed comfortable with the materials and concepts, and the stress level was very low at this point in the classroom. The 50-minute period, or "C" day, was the following Friday, and the students were asked to teach the lesson for which they would be responsible to each other. My plan called for 16 students to teach the first two lessons to the children one week, and the other 15 students to teach the final two lessons the following week. The class was divided in half into a Week One Team, which would teach the first two lessons, A and B, and a Week Two Team, which would teach the last two lessons, C and D. The Week One Team was divided further into subgroups of lessons A and B, as was the Week Two Team, which formed subgroups for lessons C and D. Each student was paired with another student from the same week, but with the opposite lesson. Each student was to teach the basic parts of the lesson and obtain feedback from his/her partner. A guided worksheet was provided so that students could note their own strengths and weaknesses before teaching in the elementary classroom (appendix B). I was hopeful that all students would have a chance to review both lessons that they would be teaching in the following weeks.

I realized the time line would be short, approximately 25 minutes per lesson per student. But I expected that these high school students would have fewer questions and behave better than three elementary students would and, thus, probably could complete the bulk of the lesson in that time frame. On reflection I believe that students could have used more time for practice teaching. (I was also out of the building on the day they taught each other, and although I had an excellent substitute, the students did not make the best use of their class time.)

Teaching

After the preparation for teaching, a student leader was appointed for each day that the Shorewood students would travel to Parkwood. This person was responsible for getting the lab materials and any additional supplies to the elementary school and returning them to the high school at the end of the day. The Shorewood students provided their own transportation and were allowed the full 100 minutes for travel time, to set up the labs at the elementary school, and to teach the lessons.

When the high school students went to the elementary classrooms, they were divided into smaller groups of approximately eight students, with each smaller group entering an elementary class of 24 children. For consistency, the groups of eight remained the same and stayed with their three assigned children for both lessons that week. The elementary students called the high school students their "senior buddies." The half of the class that remained behind worked on a group project that required the same two weeks for completion. At the end of the two-week period, each group of three elementary children had worked with two "senior buddies," one from each week of lessons.

The high school students were greeted at Parkwood each day by the elementary teachers. Laboratory materials were set up, and the high school students conducted their teaching. My student teacher also attended these sessions and videotaped the activities in both classrooms. As displayed on the videos, the elementary students were very excited that their "senior buddies" were visiting. They were eager to learn, and the high school students had an almost instant rapport with these children. Each classroom was very busy, and the 1:3 ratio of teacher to students was ideal in terms of providing support, engagement, and monitoring.

Evaluation

The follow-up consisted of four different activities to evaluate the effectiveness of this unit and triangulate the data.

a. A questionnaire was completed by the elementary teachers that focused on the preparedness and behavior of my students in their building (appendix C). This instrument had two intents. It kept my students accountable for their behavior and gave me feedback on the elementary teachers' perceptions of this project after each teaching session.

b. A questionnaire was completed by high school students, elementary teachers, and me to explore what the value of this unit was for the high school students.

c. The high school students were asked to write a reflective paper concerning their preparation for this unit, the actual teaching of the unit, and their attitudes about the value of this unit as an educational experience for them.

d. The elementary students provided a "gallery walking tour" for the high school students to show them the journals, puppet shows, dioramas, plays, and posters they had created after learning about whales from their "senior buddies." The "gallery" display demonstrated to the high school students what the Parkwood students had learned during the project.

Findings and Analysis

The elementary teachers were very positive about the value of this project. Cathi Wrolstad felt that "it was a very worthwhile project and one we would like to keep going next year!" The request was made by both elementary teachers to have more teaching sessions between the schools. Chuck Orser wrote that we could improve the project by "having more sessions. I had some kids who are not normally motivated asking when they [Shorewood students] were coming." Ms. Wrolstad noted, "If you could afford the time, I would like your kids to work with our kids more. As relationships developed, learning increased."

From my perspective, it was wonderful to see the connections we made between high school "teachers" and their students. I also gained a new respect for the very busy and difficult job of an elementary teacher and for the incredibly gifted teachers with whom I had the pleasure to work. In addition, the project provided me with a better understanding of the types of major science concepts taught at the elementary level and how these can be developed within a K–12 science curriculum.

From the questionnaire in appendix C, which was completed by the elementary teachers, I learned that in all cases the high school students were prepared, worked well independently, were good role models, and were helpful to the younger students. They had some trouble arriving on time for two of the four lessons, mostly during the second week, and the main suggestion for improvement was to allow more opportunities for high school students to teach elementary students.

Questionnaires

As described above, I developed three questionnaires using criteria articulated by my students that identified the ingredients in valuable educational experiences. Each questionnaire used a four-point scale, with 4 meaning "strongly agree" and 1 meaning "strongly disagree."

The responses of the Shorewood students on their questionnaires were overwhelmingly positive, with average scores above 3.0 on all but 3 of 20 items (appendix D). Of the three statements that did not rate a 3 or higher, two had average scores that approached 3: statement 3, 2.71: "I found this project to be personally challenging;" and statement 18, 2.85: "I learned a great deal about whales from this curriculum. Only item statement 6 had a score, 1.81, that indicated disagreement: "I found this project to be difficult." Eight of the 20 items had average scores above 3.5, and the remaining 9 averages were from 3.0 and 3.5.

On their questionnaires, the elementary teachers rated all statements as either 3 or 4 (appendix F), with scores of 3 given by both teachers in the categories of providing our students with a hands-on learning situation (#2), personal challenge (#3), difficulty of the project (#6), and the project having a definite completion and reward (#7). Thirty-four of the 44 total responses on these two questionnaires were 4.

Some interesting items to note on the questionnaire were the questions asked of the elementary teachers about their perception of what the high school students learned. Both teachers agreed that the Shorewood students learned a great deal about whales (#18), community involvement (#19), and interacting with younger students (#20). Both felt the project was educationally valuable for the high school students (#17).

The high school teacher's questionnaire was similar to the other two. I found that I strongly agreed in almost all categories that the students were having a valuable educational experience. However, I also agreed with my students' relatively weak agreement with statement 3, amount of personal challenge, and disagreement with item statement 6, difficulty of the project. My conclusion is that if I run a project like this again, I want to be sure that its activities are more academically challenging for the high school students and, thus, more difficult.

Student Journals

The journal writing done by the high school students was intended to gather data in three categories: the value of the students' preparation to teach; students' attitudes about the concepts they taught; and students' judgments of the value of the cross-age teaching experience. Eighteen students wrote responses in their journals, and I found the following:

- Thirteen students found the experience to be valuable to them.
- Thirteen students wanted more background information.
- Seven students requested more preparation time for laboratory set up and supplies.
- Three mentioned enjoying the IMAX film.
- One student claimed the material was too simple.
- Four students noted the block schedule as the reason why such a project could take place.

One student wrote:

> It was nice to see the students happy and eager to learn about whales. In my opinion, we should share our knowledge with people younger then we are. The students at Parkwood gained some facts of whales, while we gained experience in teaching. I also learned more about whales. Just like in math class, by teaching a problem to another student, you, too, will have a better understanding.

Another student noted:

Teaching the kids was fun, but it seemed like some of the concepts were too advanced for children that young. They understood that a big whale could stay warmer than a small whale, but they did not understand why except that the whale was either big or small. Measuring the temperatures of the water was also something that took a lot of time and may not have been worth it. The children became sidetracked very easily during the five minutes between each measurement. I feel this experience was valuable to the Parkwood kids. I had fun doing it, but I really did not get that much out of it.

These comments illustrate two different responses from Shorewood students. The first focuses on the benefit of learning gained from teaching. The second notes that the student was not challenged academically by this activity, although she did see the value of her efforts as a teacher of young children. Another student explained this second perspective more directly: "For us, this was an opportunity to learn about teaching, not about science." For many students, this may have been where the real challenge lay in this project. Another student explained:

The interaction with the Parkwood kids was great. Both the kids and the teachers learned a lot, more than we would normally, anyway. I think that getting young kids interested in animals and the environment is very important and valuable. Also, giving older high school students the responsibility of teaching is a very good thing.

Another student, a reticent teacher who wanted more preparation time and worried about not having enough teaching examples, stated:

I feel this was a good learning experience, not academically, but it was just a good experience. I learned how to teach someone something. I learned how it feels to be a teacher and how it is to get concepts across to students. I know now that I've helped someone who will carry it [the concepts] with them for the rest of their life.

After reading 13 similar journal entries, I am convinced that these students were having a valuable educational experience, and that they were learning valuable skills that they will retain throughout their lives.

"Gallery Walking Tour"

The final evaluation tool I used in determining the effects of this project was my observation of the elementary and high school students interacting on a "gallery walking tour" held at Shorewood High School. The Parkwood students arrived by bus, carrying with them 10 dioramas, 13 posters, 2 videotapes, 3 puppet shows, and a number of journals and books, all created in response to their study of whales. The elementary students set up their displays in the Marine Biology classroom, and the high school students, administrators, and my student teacher and I took a walking tour through the various projects, stopping to ask questions of the students responsible for a particular piece of work and to admire their creations. The communication among all the participants was wonderful to watch.

As I talked with Chuck Orser, he noted that one of his most stubborn and difficult students, who had been unwilling to turn in work all year, had completed a complex diorama for his "senior buddy." In another case I noticed one of our seniors with high anxiety about this project and low self-esteem working with some of the more difficult children very successfully, a large smile on her face as she was escorted around the room by her elementary friends. The high school students then provided a tour of Shorewood to the Parkwood students, who will attend Shorewood eventually, and everyone gathered in the cafeteria for a cupcake and ice cream party provided by the "senior buddies." The elementary students were not eager to leave, as explained in a journal comment of one Shorewood student:

> The kids were rambunctious, which is expected at that age, but it made it tougher on us to teach. Still, it was enjoyable at the same time, too, because they (at least one of my kids) got attached to us literally, which made it hard to leave. It was like leaving a brother or a sister.

After watching the interactions among all the students and evaluating the projects produced by the Parkwood children for the gallery tour, I am convinced this project was advantageous to both schools. Parkwood gained role models and mentor teachers for the elementary students, and the Shorewood students became valued, if temporary, members of that school's community, took on teaching responsibilities, and enhanced their own self-esteem in the process.

Action Plan

When I reflect on the four basic parts of this project, I see definite changes I will make next year to improve some areas of the project and to strengthen the parts already in place and working effectively. In the first activity, the introduction to the elementary students, we were fortunate to have had an event that was local, fun for all classes, and relevant to the topic. An introductory gathering for students from both schools was seen as a good start to this project by all of the teachers and most of the students involved. However, communication time was limited, and the connections between students in the different schools could have been made more meaningful. If the teaching staff at both schools met and assigned "senior buddies" to groups before the introductory meeting, this would allow the introductory meeting time to be used in a more purposeful manner. The students could then make a connection with their tutor/tutees and begin to build relationships. The *Whales* IMAX movie may not be in town, but a substitute film shown at Shorewood or perhaps a trip to and a scavenger hunt at the aquarium might be a better start and provide more interaction between the groups.

The teaching activity appeared to go well in the view of the Parkwood teachers and students. However, many of the Shorewood students requested more time to prepare for teaching and to become familiar with laboratory setup. This request was a result of too little preparation time in the schedule and the limited value of the 50-minute period during which students had to practice their teaching skills. I will allow them at least one additional 100-minute period to review the lessons, and I will hold them accountable by having them present their lesson as a group of eight to the class. This will include setting up their own materials and packing what they need to take to Parkwood.

The other request from my students was to teach them more detailed information about whales and to provide them with more examples that they could use in their own teaching at Parkwood. I will respond to these requests, and to the critique of some students about the lack of academic challenge in this project, by devoting at least another week of class time to a more thorough and demanding study of whales within the context of the Marine Biology course. I may also accept the suggestion of one student and develop and implement a few quizzes about this study, which will help to hold the students accountable.

Finally, we all enjoyed the form of assessment provided by the Parkwood students in their projects and presentations. The highlight for these students was arriving at Shorewood and being allowed to spend an afternoon where their "senior buddies" went to school. In light of the value of students presenting their work to an audience, another improvement I will make in this project involves creating a presentation that Shorewood students can give as part of this effort. I have a pattern for a life-size whale that would take about two weeks to build, the same time frame that it takes to teach the unit at Parkwood. While half the class was teaching at Parkwood, the other half could build a whale. The Parkwood students could then walk through the model during their visit to Shorewood. In future years, as technological capacity increases in my classroom, perhaps we can monitor the migration of whales or present our own reports on special interests of Shorewood students in whale-related topics. These innovations would increase the academic challenge for Shorewood students in this project.

My final judgment about this project is this: Although the academic learning that my students gained from their efforts was probably not as much as I had hoped, they learned significant information about whales. In addition, they learned a good deal about teaching and about responsibility for their interactions with younger children. When I asked one student if such a project should be included in a science curriculum or if it were more community service learning and belonged in a different class, he said, " Yes, it is community service learning, but I feel that any time you can relate what you are learning to the community it is beneficial, and such a project should not only be included in a science course, but in every course." If I continue this project next year as I hope to do, my commitment will be to enhance the academic component for my students and to use my learning from this year to enhance the process of cross-age teaching.

One of the same students I quoted above summed up this effort insightfully.

> I thought the experience was very valuable. I learned and relearned several things about whales, especially when we saw the IMAX film. Obviously, there won't be an IMAX film about whales every year, but having something like that built in where even the high schoolers learned new things about whales was a good idea, The Parkwood children learned quite a lot about whales, and, based on my own memories of elementary school, I think they will be likely to remember what they learned for a longer time because it was taught to them in a unique environment.

Another student offered the following conclusions about the value of this cross-age tutoring experience:

> The most valuable part for us was that we were given the opportunity and independence to prepare and present a lesson where we were the ones in charge of its fate, of whether it would be good or bad, not just the teacher. No matter what someone does after high school, be it a job or further school, it will be important to be able to carry out projects and present them or perform duties with a high level of independence and skill, and anything like this project that helps lay the foundation for doing that is valuable. Also, many teenagers do not often get to be in a situation where they are looked up to and respected because they have something important to teach to someone else.

Appendix A

The following is a list of experiences that the Marine Biology students at Shorewood high school felt were "valuable" and why that experience was seen as unique.

1. Riding a bike—inspired by practice and motivation from other children

2. Spanish—watching a foreign film and being able to understand the language, relevancy

3. Basketball—an unforeseen injury forced improvement due to more attention given to the problem

4. Parallel parking—skill needed to obtain a driver's license, inspired by motivation

5. Learning to swim—in Hawaii, inspired by older brother

6. Learning to surf—inspired by friends in marine biology course in Hawaii

7. Mathematics—inspired by desire to learn on your own

8. Left-handed lay-up in basketball—achieved by practice and with the help of friends

9. Experiments with sound—achieved knowledge through trial and error, inspired by desire to create a product or synthesize music

10. Flags—ability to do specific maneuver, achieved with the help of friends and practice

11. Snowboarding—achieved by practice and lessons, motivated by friends

12. Waterskiing—a family activity, involved practice and motivation

13. State DECA Award—relevancy of what was learned in school to real life

14. Fifth grade notebooks—high expectations needed to be met, continue to use that skill

15. Golf—decreasing score and learning to improve, coached by friends and other valued golf players

16. Jumping on horseback—challenging, took practice and instruction

17. Manual shift driving—inspired by desire to learn, friends coached and taught

18. Visit to Berlin—amazed at the way people worked together

19. Freshman year was memorable—due to the presence of many friends old and new

20. Realizing how atoms work—occurred in the fourth or fifth grade, making sense of ideas

21. Learning to helicopter on snow skis—learning and then being able to teach a class

22. A trip to Australia—learned a lot about self and others

23. Jumping off side of washing machine and discovering he was not Superman—painful consequences made it memorable

24. Sailing—enjoying a trip with family and friends while learning new techniques

25. Denmark trip—learned relevant information about another country and self

Descriptive words from discussion with students of what made their educational experience valuable:

practice	desire to learn	helpful	hands-on
enthusiasm	fun	sensory	participation
hard work	useful	entertaining	cooperative
rewards	applicable	motivating	challenging

Appendix B

Please have this form checked off before leaving today.

Peer Teaching Assignment
Marine Science/per. 6

Directions

1. Teach and/or discuss your whale lesson(s) with a partner from a different group for 15 to 20 minutes.
2. Debrief with your partner for 5 to 10 minutes, following the guidelines below.
3. Switch roles and repeat steps 1 and 2.

Remember, As group with Bs, and Cs group with Ds.

Guidelines for Self-Evaluation

1. List three things that went well with your lesson.

2. List three things you will work on before teaching the lesson to Parkwood students.

3. Please list all the materials you will need to teach this lesson.

Appendix C

Evaluation of Shorewood "Student Teachers"

Group Letter (A–D) _____ Names _____

_____

_____

_____

Please provide the following feedback on the Shorewood students.

1. Did the students arrive on time?

   _____

   _____

2. Were students properly prepared with materials?

   _____

   _____

3. Were students properly prepared with information?

   _____

   _____

4. Did the students interact independently with the elementary students, or did they need guidance?

   _____

   _____

5. Did the students behave appropriately as role models for the younger students?

   _____

   _____

6. Were the Shorewood students helpful to the younger students?

   _____

   _____

7. I think that we could improve this next year by:

_____

_____

_____

_____

_____

_____

Additional comments (please include the names of any students who were extremely helpful and those who could have used more guidance.)

Appendix D

Marine Biology-Evaluation for High School Students

According to our classroom discussion on learning experiences and memorable moments, how would you rate the whale teaching unit in each of the following categories?

1=strongly disagree; 2=disagree; 3=agree; 4=strongly agree

					Totals	_Average_

		1	2	3	4	Average
1.	This project was a fun learning experience.	0	0	5	22	3.81
2.	This project provided me with a hands-on learning situation.	0	0	12	15	3.55
3.	I found this project to be personally challenging.	2	7	16	3	2.71
4.	This project allowed me to be involved in a group activity.	0	0	11	17	3.60
5.	I was very enthused about this project and it increased my desire to learn.	0	2	15	9	3.26
6.	I found this project to be difficult.	11	10	6	0	1.81
7.	This project clearly had a definite completion reward.	0	4	11	12	3.29
8.	I found this project provided me with useful information or experiences I will use in the future.	0	1	12	12	3.44
9.	I can apply this project to other areas of my life.	0	0	17	9	3.33
10.	I found this project to be helpful in learning about whales.	0	5	15	7	3.07
11.	I consider this to be a valuable sensory experience.	0	3	12	13	3.35
12.	I consider this to be a project that requires participation on my part.	0	0	3	20	3.86

		1	2	3	4	
13.	I found this project to be entertaining to experience.	0	0	4	19	3.83
14.	I found this project to be one that requires cooperation withing my teaching group.	0	1	5	17	3.69
15.	I found this project to be educationally motivating.	0	1	12	9	3.36
16.	I think this project should be included in the curriculum next year.	0	0	6	16	3.72
17.	I found this curriculum to be educationally valuable.	0	1	11	9	3.38
18.	I learned a great deal about whales from this curriculum.	1	5	11	4	2.85
19.	I learned a great deal about community involvement from this curriculum.	0	1	11	11	3.43
20.	I learned a great deal about interacting with younger students from this curriculum.	0	0	4	19	3.82

Appendix E

Marine Biology-Evaluation for High School Teachers Concerning the Educational Experiences of the High School Student

1=strongly disagree; 2=disagree; 3=agree; 4=strongly agree

1. This project was a fun learning experience.   1   2   3   4

2. This project provided the students with a hands-on
    learning situation.   1   2   3   4

3. The students found this project to be personally challenging.   1   2   3   4

4. This project allowed the students to be involved in group
    activity.   1   2   3   4

5. The students were very enthused about this project, and it
    increased their desire to learn.   1   2   3   4

6. The students found this project to be difficult.   1   2   3   4

7. This project clearly had a definite completion and reward.   1   2   3   4

8. This project provided students with useful information or
    experiences that can be used in the future.   1   2   3   4

9. The students can apply this project to other areas of their lives.   1   2   3   4

10. This project is helpful in learning about whales.   1   2   3   4

11. I consider this to be a valuable sensory experience.   1   2   3   4

12. I consider this to be a project that requires participation
    on the part of the students.   1   2   3   4

13. I found this project to be entertaining to experience.   1   2   3   4

14. I found this project to be one that requires cooperation
    within the student teaching group.   1   2   3   4

15. This project is educationally motivating.   1   2   3   4

16. I think this project should be included in the curriculum
    next year.   1   2   3   4

17. I feel this curriculum is educationally valuable.   1   2   3   4

18. The students learned a great deal about whales from   1   2   3   4
    this curriculum.

19. The students learned a great deal about community   1   2   3   4
    involvement from this curriculum.

20. The students learned a great deal about interacting with   1   2   3   4
    younger students from this curriculum.

21. I found this program to be academically valuable to my   1   2   3   4
    students in teaching about whales.

22. I found this program to be educationally valuable to my   1   2   3   4
    students as a community service project.

Appendix F

Average scores for both teachers

Marine-Biology-Evaluation for Elementary Teachers Concerning the Educational Experiences of the High School Student

1=strongly disagree; 2=disagree; 3=agree; 4=strongly agree

1. This project was a fun learning experience.   1   2   3   <u>4</u>

2. This project provided the students with a hands-on learning situation.   1   2   <u>3</u>   4

3. The students found this project to be personally challenging.   1   2   <u>3</u>   4

4. This project allowed students to be involved in a group activity.   1   2   3   <u>4</u>

5. The students were very enthused about this project, and it increased their desire to learn.   1   2   <u>3</u>   4

6. The students found this project to be difficult.   1   2   <u>3</u>   4

7. This project clearly had a definite completion and reward.   1   2   <u>3</u>   4

8. This project provided students with useful information or experiences that can be useful in the future.   1   2   <u>3</u>   4

9. The students can apply this project to other areas of their lives.   1   2   3   <u>4</u>

10. This project is helpful in learning about whales.   1   2   3   <u>4</u>

11. I consider this to be a valuable sensory experience.   1   2   3   <u>4</u>

12. I consider this to be a project that requires participation on the part of the students.   1   2   3   <u>4</u>

13. I found this project to be entertaining to experience.   1   2   3   <u>4</u>

14. I found this project to be one that requires cooperation within the student teaching group.   1   2   3   <u>4</u>

15. This project is educationally motivating.   1   2   3   <u>4</u>

16. I think this project should be included in the curriculum next year.   1   2   3   <u>4</u>

17. I feel this curriculum is educationally valuable.   1   2   3   <u>4</u>

18. The students learned a great deal about whales from   1   2   3   <u>4</u>
    this curriculum.

19. The students learned a great deal about community   1   2   3   <u>4</u>
    involvement from this curriculum.

20. The students learned a great deal about interacting with 1   2   3   <u>4</u>
    with younger students from this curriculum.

21. I found the students to be beneficial to my classroom   1   2   3   <u>4</u>
    as role models.

22. I found these students to be beneficial as educational   1   2   3   <u>4</u>
    teaching assistants.

PART 3

Structural Innovation and Professional Development in the Block Period

8

Student Attitude and Motivation in a Block Period High School Program with a Two-Year Integrated Curriculum

Marianne Winter Lang
Tahoma High School

Marianne Winter Lang teaches in both a two-year *looping* Integrated Program in which English, science, and social studies are interconnected, and in a traditional high school structure of separate, unrelated courses. In the Integrated Program she and her team colleagues teach the same 90 students for ninth and tenth grades. She wanted to explore more formally "whether student attitude and motivation was in fact better due to being in an every-other-day, full-day, two-year block as opposed to traditional ninth and tenth grade English classes that were just one of six on the students' schedules."

Her findings confirm her hypothesis: "The students in the Integrated Program are more motivated by the curriculum, and to the extent possible for a teenager, they enjoy school. They value connections, they are not confined by content barriers, and they write and think across the curriculum."

Introduction and School Description

For the past decade, Tahoma High School, located in a rapidly growing rural/suburban community 20 miles southeast of Seattle, has pursued school reform actively. Changes have included a 30-minute daily reading period, a senior project, block periods on an alternating day schedule, and an integrated curriculum.

As we prepared for the change to block periods, our staff spent a year of in-service experimenting with new instructional strategies for extended class periods. Along with the new strategies and the decision to change to 100-minute periods came flexibility within a day that lent itself easily to subject integration. Over the years that the faculty has taught in block periods, we have moved out of the isolation of content-specific departments and into stimulating discussions and experiments with integrated curriculum. We also began the planning for a two-year, ninth and tenth grade Integrated Program for 90 students and three teachers, one each from English, social studies, and science. As we planned our Integrated Program, our goal was to link the past and future experiences of students and bridge ideas between content areas. We hoped to raise student awareness of the fact that life is an intricate web of connections. Our district outcomes expressed our belief that all students should become complex thinkers, self-directed learners, community contributors, quality producers, collaborative workers, and effective communicators as a result of their education.

We are currently in our fourth year of the Integrated Program. I was fortunate enough to be a part of the program from its inception. Prior to its start, the three teachers who would be teaching in the program spent an entire year planning with administrators, curriculum directors, and department heads. With the help of our curriculum director, Nancy Skerritt, we identified the essential content from ninth and tenth grade English, Washington State history, health, earth science, and biology. We then organized the content around themes and incorporated thinking skills and culminating projects. After the pilot group of ninth graders had completed the first year, the students and teachers moved to tenth grade together, and a new ninth grade team was started. For this school year, we had three teams and nine teachers working in the Integrated Program. Next year we will increase the program to four teams, two at each grade level.

Tahoma High School's schedule consists of a six-period structure in which the students attend three 100-minute periods each day. Thus students in the Integrated Program meet all day, every other day. In the program, the day is divided into large-group instruction and activities for all 90 students, and three 30-student rotation periods. The all-day schedule provides flexibility for guest speakers, field trips, and varied classroom activities. The same group of students stays together with the same teachers for two years. The students were selected randomly for the first four years of the program, but as of this spring the Integrated Program was open to those who registered for it. The Integrated Program is not an honors or gifted class. We have a wide range of ability and achievement levels, including our fair share of special education students. In the future, students will be able to select through open enrollment whether they want to be in the Integrated Program or the traditional program.

The building administration and the curriculum office have collected data throughout the evolution of the Integrated Program. The data compare Integrated students to their class as a whole in attendance, discipline referrals, standardized test scores, attitude, and grades. The Tahoma School District does a nice job of piloting projects without rushing into changes too quickly. Feedback is collected so we can assess the program, answer questions from parents and administrators, and change and refine the program. Although most of the quantitative data have supported the Integrated Program, the most convincing evidence for me is both my own feelings about the program and our students' highly positive feelings. This is why action research appeals to me. I can discuss how I feel and how students feel about the education they are experiencing.

My first group of ninth and tenth graders just graduated, and I was amazed at how often they stopped by to talk with me about how much they liked Integrated. They valued both the education they received and the connections they made with the teachers and each other. In fact, as they prepared to graduate this spring, they wanted to get together one last time. We held a reunion at which we watched videotape footage of them as ninth and tenth grade students returning their learning logs and portfolios. Attendance and feedback were outstanding, and the reunions will become a tradition. The fact that these seniors saw the value of the education they received led me to wonder whether students saw the benefits of this program only at some distance from it, or if the tenth graders themselves were aware of the benefits of a more integrated education.

Description of the Research Question

One of the most interesting aspects of my research is that, although I have been involved with the Integrated Program for three periods during each of the last four years, I also have taught two traditional English classes on the nonintegrated days. The combination of traditional and integrated curriculum has provided fertile ground for comparison. Last year, when I had ninth graders for Integrated, I also had a traditional ninth grade English class. This year, my Integrated students were in tenth grade, and I also taught a tenth grade English class with five of the same students I had last year in my traditional English 9 course.

As a whole, the tenth graders in my traditional English class did not appear to be as motivated or interested in learning and achievement as students of the same age in the two-year Integrated social studies, science, and English class. This could be the result of differences between these two groups of students, but more likely it is because the integrated structure provides a more stimulating environment for learning, which raises the achievement level for all types of students.

In the traditional classes during both years, nonachievers have set the tone, and it was not "cool" to be an achiever. Consequently, the "A" students quietly went about their business without calling attention to themselves. In contrast, because the learning in the Integrated Program was interconnected, almost all of the students became actively involved in the life of the class. The Integrated class, with its curriculum's inclusion of real-life issues, made sense to the learners, thereby engaging low and high achievers. We had no primary texts; the newspaper was a constant resource. The Integrated Program motivated students to learn because they felt more connected to the teachers **and** the content.

Over the past four years I have often wondered if the students in the traditional classes felt disjointed because they took six seemingly unrelated courses. I also have wondered whether the Integrated students appreciated the strengths of the program. Being a part of both programs, I was able to see the distinct differences clearly. I hoped to gain more understanding of these differences through my research.

By looking at the significant differences between the traditional and Integrated programs, I hoped to validate my belief that subject integration contributes to improving student attitudes toward learning and achievement. *The question I set out to answer was whether student attitude and motivation was better due to being in an every-other-day, full-day, two-year block as opposed to traditional ninth and tenth grade English classes that were just one of six on the students' schedules.* My subjects included the students in my traditional tenth grade English class, five of whom I had also taught last year in ninth grade English, and the integrated tenth graders I had worked with for nearly two years.

Data Collection and Results

Description of Classroom Environment

To begin my data collection, I had each of my classes brainstorm lists of the characteristics of positive and negative classroom environments. The positive lists from each class were similar: respect for others, desire to be there, collaborative activities, effective use of time, valuable information/learning, discussions, and good teacher. So were the negative lists: boring, bad teacher attitude, hard teacher who doesn't explain content well, no relevance, busywork homework, pacing, and discipline problems.

After the brainstorming, I asked my students to write a paragraph describing the environment of our class. Even though students in the traditional tenth grade class tended to be more negative than the Integrated students, their comments were more positive than I had expected. They liked the class and generally found it interesting. It was the last period of the day, however, so several students commented that they were tired and wanted to go home. The majority reported that they got along well with each other and, for the most part, they treated others with respect. They did recognize that some students were loud and disruptive, making it difficult for others to learn. One student noted, "If I was a teacher in this class I would be really frustrated and I probably wouldn't be able to stand it." I was glad to see that someone empathized! Another wrote, "Most of the kids don't want to be here so they don't try. Personally, I feel frustrated. I feel that the teacher has to spend time controlling the kids who don't want to be here, and they should be put in study hall or something." The achieving students shared my frustration that off-task students inhibited learning, but they did not seem willing to do anything about it. They simply accepted the situation. An omission of significant interest to me was that so few mentioned what they were learning. They found the social situation to be far more important than anything else.

Overall, I found the traditional tenth grade students' comments to be somewhat shallow. Of primary concern for many was whether their friends were in the class and that "the teacher was fun, creative and understanding." They saw fellow students as problems, but they did not seem concerned that learning time was wasted. They saw school as a series of time periods they had to endure to reach the end of the day. I concluded that because they did not value the learning or connect it to anything relevant in their lives, they valued their feelings about the teacher and their relationships with other students far more than anything else.

In their description of the classroom environment, only two of the 30 students surveyed mentioned that they valued what they were learning. The others did not seem to see learning as a component of a positive classroom climate. Part of this undoubtedly is a function of their age. However, I also must accept some blame. I did not work as hard at making curricular connections for these students, because the opportunities to make connections made possible in the Integrated class simply did not exist in the traditional class. Throughout their day, students in the traditional program saw three teachers who had no idea what the others were doing. Most likely, their learning seemed superficial to them, so their evaluation of my class was equally shallow. Actually the student responses mirrored my feelings about the class: the traditional class simply did not have the richness or layers of an Integrated class, even though the students were acquiring the same English skills.

When I asked the Integrated tenth graders to respond to the same prompt, I was struck initially by the similarities of their responses to those of my traditional students. So much of high school is related to the teenage experience: students like to be with their friends, they want a teacher who is friendly and creative, and they have the seemingly obligatory attitude that school is sometimes boring. Beyond the commonalties, however, I found that the Integrated students were more aware of the purpose of their education. They also wrote longer and more articulate paragraphs. Many commented on active learning strategies and working in groups as positives. They discussed teaching style, content, and the relevance of the class to life and their future. For example, one student wrote, "I think even if the class is boring, it doesn't seem that way because of the different ways we learn it." Another commented, "The teacher has more than one teaching style so others can learn what the teacher is teaching." The students enjoyed and valued specific activities such as speaking in front of the class and discussing issues. "Even though English is not my favorite subject," one explained, "the teacher always has a positive outlook on the class, and that helps motivate us. I like that we can voice our opinions and talk about all things respectfully."

After spending time comparing the two groups, I realized that the Integrated students viewed their comments to me as valuable. They wrote more and were more specific. They earnestly wanted to provide data for my research. The classroom culture was very different from a traditional classroom. I attribute that to the team building we do at the beginning of the Integrated Program. I also enjoyed teaching the Integrated class more than the traditional class, which must have had an impact on my effectiveness. Even though the content was similar to traditional English 10, I used different strategies and activities in the Integrated Program, creating two distinct worlds of learning. Thus, in the Integrated Program, students were less aware of content boundaries. A student explained, "They say it [English] is integrated with science and social studies, but what it really is is three classes doing the same topic." I don't know if this particular student meant this to be positive or negative, but to me it showed that we are accomplishing what we set out to do. Another student pulled it all together:

> I think this class has a very good environment that makes it easier to learn. Part of it, I think, is because we have been with these people for a long time so we are all pretty relaxed around each other, and it is not as intimidating as other classes to talk in front of the class. I think that everyone has a pretty good attitude and respects everyone. Even if they don't like this subject, pretty much everyone pays attention because you teach us in so many different learning styles.

This student's observation validated all of my efforts in the Integrated Program.

Student Survey: Traditional English 10 Results

After my students had described the classroom environment, I developed a survey (appendix A) designed to gather their perceptions of the value of English, 100-minute periods, and integrated education. The students in the traditional English 10 program recognized that they were learning and practicing skills such as punctuation, essay format, reading, writing, grammar, and understanding literature. They also felt that I, as their teacher, cared: "My teacher is very nice and she cares about grades in the class. However, a lot of people do not care about grades, but she still cares." What they were not clear about was the value of the class in relation to their future. Several mentioned that resume writing would help, and some thought English 10 would help with eleventh and twelfth grade and the senior project. Yet, one student wrote in response to the question regarding the value of the class, "It depends on what you want to do in the future." This comment illustrates how this student saw the purpose of the class and its relationship to his future. This attitude was common among these students, although one student did note, "Writing and speech are important in all jobs." In contrast, the Integrated students' responses, discussed below, showed that they were far more aware of various kinds of connections within their classes and between the Integrated class and their lives.

The block periods were praised by both groups. One student in the traditional class wrote, "The 100-minute periods are more relaxed, and it is more like a family than a classroom full of kids, but it is hard to focus after a while." Most students in the traditional class felt the longer periods reduced stress because there was more time for one-on-one interaction and help. Another aspect valued was that the rotating daily schedule gave them two days to complete their homework. Most agreed that the teachers could cover more "stuff" and had more time for activities.

In addition to the survey, I asked the five students I'd had last year—Barney, David, Jason, Nikki, and Meaghan—if they felt any benefit from having the same teacher for English two years in a row. Barney said that he didn't think it made much of a difference. Jason and David said that it was good because they knew my teaching style and expectations. Nikki and Meaghan felt it had a huge impact. Meaghan commented, "Yes, I think it made a world of difference having the same teacher, because I was already used to your teaching style and just being around you made me remember things from the previous year that I might have forgotten if I had another teacher." Meaghan's response supported my own beliefs about the value of teachers having students for two years. Over time, the teachers in our Integrated Program have found that the relationship between students and teachers is more important to the success of the program than curriculum content, and that deeper, more significant learning is made possible because of the learning environment built by these relationships. Therefore, it was interesting that this student, who was not in the Integrated Program but by chance happened to be in my class for two years, confirmed my beliefs about the importance of relationship in any learning environment.

Student Survey: Grade 10 Integrated Program Results

The most striking element of the Integrated students' surveys was the global perspective the students conveyed. They were aware of the skills they had learned and mentioned the same skills as their peers in the traditional class. However, they also listed thinking skills and public speaking, which are important aspects of the Integrated Program. As with the descriptive paragraph, the Integrated students wrote more than their peers in the traditional program. The Integrated students valued a solid English education because it "broadens and expands minds." One stated, "Writing and reading are the most important skills a person could have." In addition to an overall awareness of the value of an English class, they were far more conscious of the links to their future. The Integrated students saw the world as interconnected. As a result, they saw English skills as being valuable everywhere, not just in particular careers: "All writing skills will help me, because no matter what job I get, I guarantee I will need good writing skills." One student said, "People judge you on grammar, and you use the skills all the time." Another wrote, "English is probably the most important class because it teaches things that relate to life, not like math or history." One student really saw the big picture: "Everything you learn in high school, from friends to homework, will help you in life." In sum, the Integrated students saw the larger framework of learning, while the traditional students merely saw the skills. Our goal with the Integrated Program was to guide students in making connections to the world around them, and these comments validated our efforts.

As with most of the teachers and students in the school, the Integrated students also highly favored 100-minute periods. Their comments revealed the strengths of block periods:

> "It gives me a better attitude toward each class because I don't get too sick of it because we don't have the same classes every day."

> "You can get more help, but sometimes it drags on."

> "Longer periods have more learning, the more learning the smarter you get."

> "It is easier to learn when you don't feel rushed."

> "Teachers can start and end an activity in one day instead of having it carry over from one day to the next."

> "We get more accomplished and do more in-depth projects and assignments."

> "I am normally really shy and I don't like to talk, but the long periods help me feel more comfortable around people so I will ask more questions."

> "A teacher has more time with the extended period to help out students with troubles and teach more besides just doing work."

As a strong supporter of block periods, I was thrilled to read the students' largely positive comments.

One of the greatest benefits of our every-other-day schedule was that we had the Integrated students all day, every other day. We were able to alter the schedule to meet our needs because any changes affected only the three teachers involved in the team. We scheduled guest speakers and field trips with greater ease because of the flexibility. We have a 100-seat lecture hall at Tahoma High School, so we met in a large group every day for attendance and announcements. Often we stayed together for discussions and other activities. The rest of the day was then split into three periods in which the three groups of 30 students rotated among the three different teachers. We created our own schedule within the confines of the whole school schedule, still giving our students the same breaks and lunch as the rest of the school. We found that our students were reluctant to change their social time, and we respected that so we were committed to ensuring common social time in any schedule changes we made. I always have considered flexibility to be a great bonus of the Integrated Program. According to the students' surveys, they felt the same way about the flexibility of the schedule:

"It is not as stressful."

"Anything that needs flexibility can happen because of the Integrated Program."

"I like it when and how we can change the schedule; it makes it much more interesting. It is something to look forward to."

"It is easier to understand when three classes are blended together and to understand how they relate to life."

"You get to know the teachers better and they know you, so it is easier for them to help you learn."

"Having integrated all day is really cool. We never have to rush, and we can go at our own pace."

"Students don't feel as pushed or pressured."

"Integrated teaches us the same thing in every class, except each class has a different perspective."

"We don't really have a set schedule and that varies to what we feel like doing and to allow other ideas to branch out. It also takes the strain off of having separate classes because all of these classes are related."

"It teaches me more about working in groups, which is a skill needed to survive in the work world."

"I think being with the same people all day helps me learn because I am comfortable with everyone and we can do bigger projects and really get involved."

"It makes things easier to understand because the teachers connect all three subjects."

"It enhances learning 100 percent. It is much easier to learn with the same students for a whole year."

Through these comments, I realized that the Integrated students strongly valued both the flexibility of the schedule and the program in general. The Integrated Program has been successful because, though it has much of the same content as traditional classes, student attitude is enhanced by the relationships between adults and students and among students, the many connections among subjects within the curriculum and connections between the curriculum and students' lives, the flexibility of the schedule, and the variety of teaching styles and activities.

In my Integrated class, I also had three students who transferred into Integrated at the start of tenth grade. Lindsay moved from out of state, and Brandon and Geir had been in the traditional program, but did not feel challenged, so they transferred into the Integrated class. I was anxious to hear what they had to say about the differences they noticed between the two models of instruction. All three were glad that they had transferred into the Integrated Program. They felt that working with the same topics in three subject areas and working with the same peers made school more relaxed and more fun; these qualities also made learning easier. Geir reflected, "It is nice working with the same kids all year for projects. In other classes you need to get to know them before you can begin the project, but here we already know them." These three students also liked the flexibility of the day and the combination of large-group meetings with all 90 students and the smaller 30-student classes. Moreover, they found their learning to be more relevant to their lives. "We experience more than looking at a textbook, we do activities so the learning sticks with you. In other classes, you memorize for the test, and then it disappears from your mind," Brandon stated. The social aspect was something they enjoyed, although Geir commented, "There are a lot more group projects, which is hard for me because I am an independent worker. I have learned how to work with others better, though." He added, "It is good to be smart in here, unlike other places." This was interesting because I had Geir as ninth grader in a traditional class, and his class was very similar to my traditional tenth grade class this past year. He was one of a few motivated students, so it was fun to watch him blossom this year in a more positive environment.

As Brandon looked to next year, he expressed concern about going back to six unrelated courses for his junior year. Lindsay, however, said, "Next year will be weird, but we can make connections on our own; I am not worried about it." The interviews of Brandon, Geir, and Lindsay were so revealing that I found myself wishing I had tracked their experience for the entire year. At any rate, all three of these students saw the program as a positive change, and they were a great addition to our group.

Parent Survey

For the next phase of my research, I sent home a parent survey (appendix B) with all of the Integrated students and the five tenth graders I had taught for two years. Three of the five from the traditional English 10 class, and well over half from the

Integrated class were returned. Again, the affective benefits of the Integrated Program were evident in the parents' comments. Most of the parents of both groups said they had seen a positive change in their children's language arts skills. One wrote, "Jayson now helps me when I have English-related questions." The parents of the students in the traditional program felt that having the same teacher for two years had helped their child with confidence and skills. But like those of their children, their comments focused largely on specific skills taught in the class.

The Integrated parents raved about the benefits of the program. One mentioned, "I value the stability and ease of entering high school with the same students and teachers in a block class over two years." Another wrote, "Preparation for the workforce and the teamwork used in a two-year situation was more meaningful than separate classes." The parents shared our belief that a two-year program is beneficial for learning. One explained, "Continuing through a second year in the same class allows a student to become more relaxed and confident and more apt to step out and take risks." Parents seemed to have a good understanding of what we were trying to achieve, as one noted,

> The Integrated Program tied together different subject areas and helped to show how they relate to each other while studying one topic. This was a unique learning experience and made English appear more fun and interesting. Vindy learned a lot, while also being allowed to think on her own as well as in a group.

Parents also commented on the value of integrated education. The mother of Brandon, one of our transfer students, wrote, "The concept of integrating the subjects is great. We truly cannot say enough positive about the team of teachers, the techniques used, and, most of all, the ability to keep the students challenged." It was particularly rewarding to receive such positive parent input, because early in the program we'd had several skeptical parents who thought that what had worked for them was good enough for their children. The supportive comments confirmed my sense of the value of Tahoma's Integrated Program.

Teacher Interviews

For the final phase of my research I interviewed five teachers who have taught in the Integrated Program. All of the teachers involved teach three periods of the Integrated class on one day and then have a planning period and two traditional classes on the other day. All teams have a common conference period for planning and discussion. Every teacher whom I interviewed agreed that subject integration takes more time, but it is far better for students and, thus, more personally rewarding for teachers.

All of these teachers explained that Integrated students became aware of purpose in their learning and became accustomed to understanding the relevance of what they were learning. If something did not seem to fit, they wanted to know the purpose of an activity. They took an active role in their own education. Several of the teachers mentioned that their Integrated students were more creative and took more risks. All of the teachers agreed that these students were more aware of current events, and their education in general.

In contrast, teachers commented that students in the traditional program expected learning to be disjointed; as one teacher explained, "They [students] have an inability to see the big picture. In fact, they resist it." One science teacher commented that when she asked her biology students to write, they would complain, "This is biology, not English." Integrated students were not as confined by these boundaries. In fact, the Integrated classes often explored topics in greater depth and complexity because of their global perspectives.

On the issue of student behavior, a veteran social studies teacher commented, "As a teacher in Integrated, I have a greater understanding and knowledge of individual student needs and how to address them. In traditional classes, more kids act out, posturing for attention." Traditional classes, particularly one-semester courses, require teachers to attempt to diagnose students' needs quickly so they can hope to respond effectively. This structure places enormous pressure on teachers, and, of course, no teacher within such a structure can work effectively with all of the students as individuals. In contrast, in the Integrated program, teachers have time and context to get to know all of their students as individuals, and students get to know each other and their teachers better. As the same teacher explained, "Integrated provides a sense of community, a group within a school that gives a sense of belonging." The Integrated students do have problems, but they usually deal with them in a more positive manner because they feel and use the support of their peers and teachers.

All of the teachers commented that they worked harder because curriculum, especially elements relating to current events, was developed as we went along. Also, in working with two other teachers, it was impossible to "wing it." Everyone agreed that working collaboratively raised expectations for all participants, because "you don't want to let down the team." Also, to teach effectively in Integrated, teachers needed a broader and deeper content knowledge, because effective curriculum integration demanded a working conceptual understanding, not only of their own subject, but also of significant elements of the other two related subjects. One first-year teacher found the teaching in Integrated harder because she could not fall back on the safety of a "canned" or textbook curriculum. "Integrated forces me to be creative, which I find difficult," she explained. The lack of resources and the limited prep time did bog people down at times, but the rewards in terms of student learning and relationships with students were well worth the effort.

Summary

I had planned to compare student grades in the two groups, but as I got into the project, I realized that the groups were really too different in every way to make those numbers meaningful. Besides I wasn't really looking for that sort of achieve-ment outcome. I know that I had more Ds and Fs in my traditional class, largely due to a lack of motivation. I also had more special education students with be-havior problems in the traditional class. I often wondered if these students would have been more motivated to succeed in an Integrated two-year program.

What I wanted to examine was whether the Integrated Program was working as well as we thought it was, and, if so, why. All of my interviews and surveys sup-ported my initial belief. The students in the Integrated classes were more aware of what they were learning, they valued what they were learning, and they had more positive attitudes toward school. Our team spent many critical hours planning cur-riculum and determining essential content, but I am convinced the factors that de-termined the success of the program resided in the affective domain. The students felt safe in the Integrated environment. They respected their teachers and peers and felt respected themselves. As a result, they were able to relax and learn. More stu-dents achieved the district outcomes in the Integrated class than in the traditional class.

Through the process of action research, I realized how differently I taught each class. Even though both classes shared many of the same activities, the students in the traditional program did not have the same scaffolding or framework on which to hang their learning, so it was much less meaningful to them. The content is sim-ilar in both traditional and Integrated classes, but students in the traditional classes seem to be missing the larger picture.

Students do learn in the traditional model, and my findings do not necessarily cry out for a radical swing of the education pendulum. Some parents and teachers continue to favor the traditional model and believe it has greater value. In addition, scheduling all students—and all teachers—into an integrated block structure would be problematic. In light of the likelihood that we will continue to have traditional classes, it is my hope that my colleagues and I can incorporate more connections into the traditional program classes so students can see how the content in such classes is related to what they are learning in other classes and to other aspects of their lives.

It is logical for an English teacher to integrate with other content areas. Critical thinking, reading, and writing skills can be taught using a variety of content-specific topics. In fact, I have found that integrating subjects makes writing as-signments more meaningful to students. For example, instead of inventing an arbi-trary essay topic, students can write about a content issue that has arisen in social studies or science. Perhaps we can develop at least some of this integration between subjects in our traditional program.

The students in the Integrated Program are more motivated by the curriculum, and to the extent possible for a teenager, they enjoy school. They value connec-tions, they are not confined by content barriers, and they write and think across the curriculum. In the traditional program these connections cannot be made reliably;

thus, even though the students are learning valuable content, I believe they are missing out on the rich experience that working with three teachers and 90 student peers for two years provides. I hope the school district continues to expand and improve the program. Our Integrated model helps teenagers feel they are connected and important at a difficult point in their lives. High schools can be big, unfriendly places, but by creating an Integrated Program within the high school setting, educators can create an environment that is both academically rigorous and personally comfortable and welcoming.

Appendix A

Tenth Grade Survey

Thank you for your time. Please answer completely and honestly. You need not include your name.

What English-related skills have you mastered or practiced in the last two years?

How will what you learned in English help you in your future?

What is the value of an English requirement in ninth and tenth grade?

Describe your relationship with your teacher. Does your teacher care about how well you do in class?

In your opinion, how does the block period lend itself to your learning, achievement, and attitude?

(Integrated) How does the flexibility of an all-day class enhance learning?

Appendix B

Parent Survey

Dear Parent or Guardian:

Greetings! As the end of the year approaches, I am working on a combination self-assessment and research project comparing integrated English to the traditional ninth and tenth grade English class. I know you are very busy, but I would greatly appreciate it if you could take a few minutes to reflect on your son's or daughter's experience.

Name of your student _____

What changes and/or improvements have you seen in your student's language arts skills over the past two years?

What changes, if any, have you observed in your student's attitude regarding language arts?

What do you see as the value of your student taking English 9 and English 10?

Thank you very much for your time. I have had a great two years with these students.

Sincerely,

Marianne Winter Lang

9

The Instructional Coach's Role in Changing Instructional Practices in Block Periods

Elizabeth K. Mathewson
Tahoma School District

In her thirtieth year in public schools Liz Mathewson took on a new challenge: to invent a role called " secondary instructional coach" in which she would work with teaching colleagues who were new to the challenges of teaching in block periods. Mathewson wanted to explore how and to what extent she could support her colleagues' successful use of active learning strategies in their block period classes.

What she discovered was her ability to support and guide teachers through a variety of structures, including whole-staff sessions, district institutes, promoting networking, master teaching and team-teaching, one-on-one collaboration in curriculum planning, and both scheduled collaboration and "collaboration on the run."

In addition, through her coaching experiences with teachers from many subject areas, Mathewson was reinforced in her belief that "essential components run through all good instruction. . . . Active learning strategies are easy to imagine as useful in any classroom setting."

Introduction

The complexities of my experience as a Peace Corps volunteer in Brazil in the mid-1960s, after a three-month crash course in Portuguese, prepared me well for my loosely defined role as our school district's first secondary-level instructional coach. The two years of challenges that I encountered in Brazilian public health came to mind often this year as I sought to define my new role in education. Being conversant in my language helped. When given an opportunity to conduct an action research project centered on best practices for an instructional coach in block period schools, I was excited by the prospects for formal reflection on my new job.

In the past several years, two of our secondary schools in the Tahoma School District in Maple Valley, Washington, a rural/suburban community 20 miles southeast of Seattle, have adopted block period scheduling. Tahoma High School, a grade 9–12 program, moved first into 100-minute periods on a three-period-daily alternating schedule. Tahoma High School East, including half of the ninth grade and occupying the same campus as Tahoma Junior High, implemented the same schedule. Glacier Park School, housing all of the district's seventh graders, planned to introduce an 85-minute period structure on a four-period-daily alternating schedule this coming year. Tahoma Junior High School, with all of the district's eighth graders, planned to implement this same four-period schedule at the start of the following school year.

For three years the Tahoma School District had curriculum and instruction support personnel working directly with elementary teachers to improve instruction. With the move to block periods, the district leaders wished to support their secondary instructors as they expanded their instructional repertoires for actively engaging students in educational experiences. Block periods become monotonous when students are expected to sit passively while instructors remain the primary organizers and disseminators of content information, relying most heavily on the traditional lecture, silent reading, pen and paper tests, dittos, and films.

A teacher with 29 years' experience, I taught for 23 of those years in the Tahoma District, both in junior high and high school. I taught for two years in block periods at Tahoma High School and was part of a team of teachers selected by the principal to develop a series of inservices focused on active learning strategies prior to the high school's first year in block periods. During that first block period year, another teacher and I were given an extra planning period to support teachers in their instructional needs as they adapted to block periods. I also provided staff inservice in the writing process, oral communication process, and active learning strategies in block periods in our district and in neighboring districts.

My majors were English and social studies, and I taught English, geography, U.S. History, reading lab, and home economics to seventh and eighth graders. To high school students I taught practical writing, creative writing, poetry, all levels of required English, American literature, public speaking, and debate. I pursued innovations in my own classroom, developing processes and projects to engage students actively in making personal sense of their learning. Abhorring passive activities (an oxymoron), 10 years ago I paid a student to paint a large picture of an eagle in flight and a baby bird sitting in a nest with its gaping mouth waiting to be stuffed with regurgitated worms. I started each year reminding my students that the picture and caption contained an important concept for our classroom: "Learning is active, not passive."

I was hired for a position advertised as "secondary-level instructional support person." My direct supervisor, Nancy Skerritt, is the head of Curriculum and Instruction for the district and a person I respect for her vision, energy, and ability to make changes occur in our 5,000 student district. The task she outlined for me was to support instructors at the three secondary buildings, work on special projects selected by the principals, and be a part of the six-member Curriculum and Instruction (C and I) team for the district. The C and I team consists of two instructional coaches for our four elementary schools, one secondary instructional coach, one technology curriculum support person for K–12, a teacher in charge of special programs, and Ms. Skerritt.

According to Ms. Skerritt, my principal work site during first semester was to be the seventh grade school, as it was introducing an 85-minute block period schedule (appendix A). I had done some staff development with the teachers the previous spring to help to prepare them to teach in block periods. Though I devoted some time during first semester to the other schools, I spent a major part of each week at the Glacier Park School, working with individual teachers and organizing three of their half-day staff development in-services. Second semester I was to make the eighth grade building my principal work site. That building remained on a seven-period day with 45-minute periods, but it was slated to move into block periods at the start of the next school year. My job there was to introduce the staff to active learning instructional strategies at two half-day staff development in-services and to work with individual teachers.

Questions Driving My Research

After 29 years in the privacy and autonomy of my own richly stocked classroom, my first two months trying to define my new job were marked by considerable dissonance and ambiguity. From my discomfort rose five questions I sought to answer through this action research:

- Of the instructional approaches available to an instructional coach, which practice or combination of practices is most effective in fostering teacher adoption of new instructional strategies?
- At the secondary level, is it necessary for the instructional coach to have content area preparation similar to that of the teacher being coached?
- With how many teachers and schools is it reasonable or practical to expect an instructional coach to work?
- How important is the position of an instructional coach when schools wish to change teachers' instructional practices in block periods?
- How does an instructional coach develop rapport and trust with teachers?

Processes of Research

To conduct my investigation into effective practices for instructional coaches at the secondary level, I kept daily notes as I creatively tried a variety of approaches for connecting faculty with new instructional practices. I told teachers about the action research I was conducting and asked them directly about practices they found most effective in changing classroom instruction and student engagement. I formally interviewed 14 of the many people I worked with throughout the year. At the end of the school year I asked a fellow curriculum and instruction team member to interview six people I worked with, both instructors and administrators (appendix B), to gain more understanding of best practices for an instructional coach. The responses from the interviews are embedded in this narrative. Additionally, I recorded some typical conversations with teachers and have rendered two of these in this report to give an idea of the nature of the dialogues I had with teachers.

To assist the reader in visualizing my assignments and responsibilities at the four sites, I have included a graphic representation of my year in this position (appendix A). To construct a picture of the content of the district-sponsored institutes in assessment and instructional strategies, I include a preworkshop questionnaire I developed containing key district instructional themes (appendix C). Also included in the appendix to this report are tables of content from essential materials I shared with staff as I worked with them (appendixes D and E).

Findings

1. Of the instructional strategies available to an instructional coach, which is most effective in changing instructional practice in block periods?

Whole Staff Inservice Provider

The most common strategy used to expose teachers to new ideas is the whole-staff inservice presentation. Typically, a staff gathers before school on a student late-arrival day, after the students leave campus on an early dismissal day, or at an afternoon meeting after classes dismiss for the day. All of the presenting I do out of district, and about half of the presenting I do in my district, is before whole-staff groups. Though the 20 teachers I interviewed all felt strongly that large-group presentation is least effective, I believe a place exists for this practice as a part of the instructional coach's (IC's) tool kit. (Administrators seem to favor this approach because it is arranged quickly, implemented easily, and escaped from easily for precious office time free of interruptions.)

I conduct a large-group inservice just as I run a classroom. This provides opportunity for teachers to become students again and to practice the active learning procedures I am introducing before taking the strategies back to their own classes. I set up the inservice in blocks of time that resemble the time blocks of the school where I am instructing. At the beginning of the inservice I identify the active learning strategies we will be using during each block of time. I carefully choose the content piece on which to hang the strategies, because I want it to speak to the needs of all classroom teachers. My favorite content is a series of articles on building a community of learners. I provide a range of active learning strategies for reading, large-group discussion and small-group civil discourse, and group and solo writing activities. If time allows an opportunity during the inservice for collaborative groups of teachers to integrate the new practices into their own content-specific lessons, the experience grows more valuable.

A large-group inservice is also a place where collections of materials can be introduced and placed in the hands of teachers in one smooth operation. I provide Post-it® Notes so that as we peruse the materials together, teachers can flag items we will use that day or they can refer to later when they are designing their own lessons. Then, if I meet with individual teachers for curriculum planning after a large-group session, we can quickly access a common core of materials that support the delivery of content. All of our secondary staff have a personal copy of *The File*, a binder containing lesson strategies that support active learning in block periods, or the *Active Learning Folder*, a set of materials describing how to engage students in learning. The district has purchased copies of Merrill Harmin's book, *Inspiring Active Learning* (ASCD, 1994) for many of its teachers, and I tote to each site *Class 30 Compilation*, a collection of my favorite active learning strategies from 29 years as a classroom teacher (appendixes D and E).

Some teachers are such autonomous learners that they relish road-tested ideas for the classroom to add to their repertoires. These instructors can assess the potential usefulness of a new idea for their particular discipline quickly and customize it to their purposes. The metamorphosis that occurs when teachers customize each other's ideas frequently produces brand-new ideas. I like supporting this process.

District Institute Team Teaching

The Tahoma School District's Curriculum and Instruction Department ran three institutes last year: *Integrating the Curriculum, Assessment Training Focused on Reading and Math, and Instructional Strategies*. The Assessment Institute and Instructional Strategies Institute were new. Principals chose teachers to attend, or faculty members expressed an interest in being part of these four- to six-session programs. Each session was a full day, and each institute was spread over a three-month period. Teachers attending were provided subs and credit and clock hour options; both first-year and veteran teachers were a part of these combined elementary and secondary classes of 30 participants. The classes were intended to enhance the practices of solid teachers, not to serve as a rescue mechanism for teachers in trouble.

Many hours were spent by the C and I team planning these classes and then team-teaching them. I enjoyed the stimulating collaboration in lesson design with the fine teachers from the C and I department. At first I resented the amount of time this responsibility took me away from the three buildings and what I perceived to be the primary focus of my job, working directly with teachers. However, as I interviewed participants from these institutes throughout the year for this action research project, I realized the importance of teaching at the institutes to my job as an IC. The institute formats provide teaching models and active learning strategies in thinking skills, reading, performance assessment, technology application, civil discourse, project learning, group and individual research designs, writing, and teaching probing questioning skills to teachers. The C and I team sees all of these strategies as critical for engaging students actively in learning. The most effective feature of the institutes is the provision made for teachers to select one or two new teaching methods from a menu of newly learned strategies to incorporate into their own classroom lessons. Portfolios chronicling participants' growth toward the objectives (lesson plans, student work, assessments) are compiled, and videotapes of actual instruction connected to the goals are used in eliciting constructive dialogue among institute colleagues about the new teaching practices.

Blocks of institute time are structured for participants to design lessons while institute instructors from the C and I department coach and collaborate. The teachers whom I interviewed felt that the collaborative planning time, the opportunity to view themselves teaching on video, and the conversations with teaching peers were valuable for changing their classroom instructional practices. Because I spent time in the classrooms of the secondary-level institute participants, I could help these teachers make specific connections of institute work to the content of their classrooms. I found that making these connections was particularly valuable to these teachers.

Networking and Rapport Building

Networking must be a vital part of the IC's role. At the secondary level, a faculty is usually divided into departments, and planning periods are assigned with little attempt made to encourage integration or collaboration. Several times I saw practices in one classroom that I was able to share with an instructor from another classroom. If the schedule allowed, one teacher could pop down the hall and watch a colleague using an idea for active teaching that had merit in the former teacher's classroom. I reminded staff that principals had budgets to allow teachers to spend time in other secondary buildings for the day either in district or out. I also read professional materials and then introduced these materials to appropriate teachers. Knowing something about the hierarchy in the central office, I was able to connect teachers to resources and resource people, after-school classes, and institutes.

An IC is in an ideal position to share ideas from teacher to teacher. I carefully watched practices that instructors used to engage students actively in their classrooms. When a particular idea impressed me with its applicability to other classrooms, I asked the author's permission to make copies, attach the author's name and school, and share the idea with others in my travels. One instructor's interview commented:

> The IC built rapport whenever she recognized and validated one teacher's idea and asked to share it with other teachers. This helped us feel good about what we were doing in our own classes and, therefore, more willing and able to listen to ideas from others' classes or from the IC.

In September I asked teachers at the seventh grade school about how I might assist them in their work. Three teachers immediately asked me to facilitate the selection and reading of novels for their literature circles as they integrated geography themes with English skills. Countless meetings and weeks later students could be seen in literature circles reading and discussing fiction set in Asia, Africa, or the Middle East and rich with themes from the geography scope and sequence. This attention to a daunting project initiated by the teachers and supported by the IC positively affected all students and six block teachers, and it improved instruction and built rapport.

A second enormous project initiated by teachers who were too busy in their classrooms to address the problem themselves was the study of eighth period. I facilitated meetings during the school year to discuss the inherent problems of the floating eighth period. In an alternating block schedule of seven subjects, an eighth period is necessary for balance. At the seventh and eighth grade schools next year, during every seven days, all students will return to each teacher once during the eighth-period time slot.

The teachers at both schools with the eight-period schedule invited me to help them with literature circles and the rotating eighth period. Our collaborative work on these projects continued throughout the school year and into the week after students were dismissed for the summer. The hours I devoted to both of these teacher-initiated projects became an important element in my experience of building rapport with teachers in these two schools.

Through teacher requests, I worked on four projects at the high school. The first project involved reformatting the eleventh grade oral history assignment to imitate the format for the senior project. Organizing and participating in meetings to write curriculum integrating U.S. History and English 11 was the focus of the second project. The third continuing special project I supported through teacher request was coordinating, developing, and designing a service learning strand at the secondary level. The fourth project focused on helping instructors plan cross-age teaching experiences for high school students working at the seventh grade school.

Assisting staff in developing teacher-initiated projects proved to be an important networking and rapport-building element in the IC's job. When their classrooms are directly affected by support provided from the district's central office, teachers feel empowered and affirmed. As a teacher in the seventh grade school informed me, "We have been trying to get our literature circles project off the ground for two years now. I'm so glad you were here to make that possible."

Master Teaching and Team-Teaching

In the interviews, master teaching (when the IC teaches to demonstrate) and team-teaching (when the IC teaches together with the regular teacher) were mentioned as two of the most beneficial services of the IC in changing instructional practice, and one that I had been reluctant to offer during the first semester. I had a misguided belief in the autonomy of an instructor's style and wanted to build teaching repertoires, but did not want to tamper with what I saw as the special blend that integrated the teacher with the students and with the content. My teaching style is a blend of creative, learner-engaged business, playfulness, and acknowledgment of, yet ready forgiveness for, counterproductive adolescent behaviors. It worked for me for 29 years, but I did not wish to foist my style upon others.

Mid-year, teachers began asking if I would mind actually teaching while they observed or played a secondary role. The opportunity to teach I loved, but I discovered the instructors saw much more than I expected they would. Upon receiving a request to teach, I allowed time for the two of us to plan the lesson together so the teacher could see the whole sequence of planning and instruction.

One first-year teacher came to me several days after we had planned and taught together and said:

> Until I saw the actual lesson being taught with my students, I had not picked up from our planning conversations the importance of the subtle processing steps a master teacher has in place. After seeing the lesson done a second time, I was able to incorporate into my own teaching some of your warm-up and framing for the lesson. I had been assuming far too much, been leaping to content too quickly without building that framework for understanding a bigger picture.

Another teacher who had asked that we work together with an especially challenging class responded in our shared reflection after the lesson:

> You were funny and friendly, but on a mission to instruct; the lesson was extremely well thought out and designed for constant momentum and engagement. With your years of teaching experience, I was surprised how much consideration and time you still took stacking into a content lesson several skills and learning. I was affirmed that liking kids and enjoying them was an important part of being an effective teacher, too.

A librarian commented, "I don't believe the important thing is for the IC to teach, but showing a willingness to teach in a variety of disciplines communicates comfort and competence and substantiates her credibility as an instructor." Such responses changed my initial attitude and encouraged me to team-teach, master teach, or just spontaneously teach when teachers asked me to do so during a classroom visit.

One-on-One Collaborator in Lesson Planning

Collaborating with instructors as they plan short lessons or long units was the most attractive part of my job as an instructional coach. This was an activity that elicited animation and synergy from teachers and which resulted in rich learning experiences for students. A second-year teacher in a U.S. History/English block class asked if we could meet at 6:15 A.M. to plan an extensive integrated study of the Civil War. (Working around the coaching schedules and zero hour classes of secondary teachers can put an IC to work both early in the morning and late in the afternoon.) I asked him if he would mind inviting the global-thinking, creative-connections librarian to join us. The three of us brainstormed boldly for over an hour and charted a richly integrated experience for his students. As we parted he said, "Man, now that's what I call fun. And that's why I can love this job." I thoroughly enjoy building *curricular submarine sandwiches* for students and can layer technology applications, writing, reading, and speaking and thinking skills into any content lesson. As mentioned earlier, so important is collaboration among teachers that we build into our institutes ample opportunity for ICs to engage in collaborative planning with teachers.

Collaboration on the Run

I have captured two conversations that depict the nature of the dialogue that occurs in collaboration on the run and in scheduled collaboration. On the run is first.

> CB met me in the hall between classes and exclaimed, "Oh, Liz, I needed to talk with you today, but my second period class starts in four minutes."

> IC: "Let me walk with you. What's up?"

> CB: "I've been wanting to deal with textbook reading differently from the way I have in the past. My kids are in a textbook two or three times a quarter is all, but I'm never happy with the way they engage in it."

> IC: "Have you thought of adapting the *Post-it® note individual reading idea* and a *small-group processing table paper format* to force more active processing of the material?"

> CB: "Tell me more; I'm not on track with you yet."

> IC: "Have your students already used that Post-it® note idea we tried as an active reading strategy at the last half-day inservice?"

> CB: "Yes."

> IC   "And I saw your kids using table papers for their group research project in the library last week. I also noticed that KC had combined a *graphic organizer* with the table paper idea. Looked pretty engaging to me."

CB: "Right! Oh, cool. So prior to assigning the chapter to read, I'd have the small groups set up table papers with the *graphic organizer* for *main idea*, then remind them to take one Post-it® note per column of print. On the Post-it® they can write a fact, question, comment, or opinion about what they've read."

IC: "Yes, and a *citation* on at least one of the Post-it®s so they practice that again and remember that citing one's source is powerful in persuasion."

CB: "And since the chapter's so long, I could even have them *jigsaw* the sections within their group or with other groups."

IC: "As closure and confirmation of what they got from their reading, you could do a quick *whip around* and hear two important ideas from each group."

(Italicized words above are active learning strategies taught at a whole-group inservice I presented at this teacher's building; see appendix F.)

CB: "Thanks, Liz; see you at lunch.

The preceding dialogue and teachable moment could not have occurred without **all** of the following elements: whole-staff inservice, staff exposure to a collection of common active learning strategies, my knowledge of CB's style and my prior observation of her work, and my visible presence at the site.

Scheduled Collaboration

The next piece of dialogue occurred during a scheduled collaboration that lasted almost an hour. I had worked with this first-year teacher five times before, and she had tried several of the strategies to which I had introduced her. During this morning meeting, we sat on the porch of her portable.

IC: "EB, seven more weeks of your first-year teaching. How are things?"

EB: "I'll never get done. In *American Expressions* I have so much content left to cover that I'm sure is not possible to cover in seven weeks."

IC: "One can cover a lot of content in seven weeks, but more important, what skills still need work for your students? I'll help you shop through the remaining content and use that as a vehicle for carrying some additional skills work."

EB: "Well, I saw on some list that they should read *Our Town*, *All My Sons*, *The Great Gatsby*, plus complete a poetry project on a poet of their choice. And I must have eight of them in two classes flunking flat. That's so embarrassing. What can I do about that?"

IC: "Have they done enough writing and reading already?"

EB: "I'd really like them to finish at least another essay. You know, the description of the poetry project sounded like it incorporated both reading and writing and a bit of memorization and speaking. And it's spring and they'd probably enjoy something lighter. I know I would; I'm so tired."

IC: "Me, too. My battery this time of year just doesn't recharge overnight. I need the slow charge of summer break. I've listed here what you've shared. Remember, sometimes we just don't get done with everything we planned, and that's OK. Let's try to select some of the content, though, and make a profitable learning experience of it. Let's look at your options for the literature part first. I'll share with you some of what I've tried, and you can customize some of that to fit your time frame. My students thoroughly enjoyed sitting in a circle on the floor reading *Our Town*, sharing the reading of parts, talking about what spoke to them in the play: no tests, no papers, no worksheets. We'd read that for part of the period, maybe 30 or 40 minutes; then they worked in pairs on the poetry project you mentioned. Eventually, I showed them films of either *All My Sons* or *Death of a Salesman*, and with one of those we constructed and shared group essays. Do you remember that format I shared with you second quarter?"

EB: "Yes, they really got into that, especially since they were only responsible for writing one of the body paragraphs, not the whole essay, and then they hung the group essay on the walls and graded each others'. I had forgotten that. And it doesn't take too long and saves me from grading another 60 individual papers. Isn't the poetry project assessment unusual, too: a wall collage and some weird thing called a poet-tea?"

IC: "Yes, the poetry project is unusual, but it does incorporate paraphrase, analysis, style imitation, biography, and memorization. Plus the collage containing all of that must be visually attractive. After the collages were posted on the wall for awhile and I'd graded them, my students, armed with herbal tea and slices of banana bread I baked, went off with their collages in groups of four to six and had a poet-tea. During a poet-tea they shared their poet's life, a favorite poem or two with interpretation, and their memorization. The idea metamorphosed when they wanted to watch *Dead Poets' Society*, and I wanted to avoid allowing them to passively watch another movie."

EB: "OK, but let's remember before you leave to discuss the movie/book review for extra credit you mentioned last time we met. I'd like it if you could come in and teach that while I watch."

IC: "I'd enjoy that opportunity, but we'll have to allow time to plan the lesson together before I come in and teach it."

This piece of our conversation captures the flavor of dialogue between two teachers with differing years of experience whose goal is to enrich instruction and engage students in their learning. The six days of training the district provided for me this year in Cognitive Coaching helped me to tailor my conversations and collaborations with teachers, and made me more deliberative and thoughtful in my interactions with them. Cognitive Coaching teaches an interactive questioning style that helps people tap into their own resources and capacities to search out solutions and approaches to the challenges they face.

2.   At the secondary level is it necessary for the instructional coach to have content preparation similar to that of the teacher being coached?

Essential components run through all good instruction. Working with teachers in science, math, art, health, geography, business law, and physical education, I never felt at a loss for finding ways to enrich the lessons they planned for their students. Active learning strategies are easy to imagine as useful in any classroom setting (appendix F). Honoring a request from math teachers to develop a math-specific list of active learning strategies, I quickly learned that similar strategies serve all classroom settings (appendix G). Pre- and postassessments of learning are effective in any discipline to demonstrate to adolescents that they really have learned something. Some teachers actually pretest student knowledge using the same test they will use as a part of postunit assessment.

Posting on the wall of a classroom guiding questions and expansive curriculum maps of units of study, then revisiting these daily while students add to them has merit in any situation. Developing checklists and rubrics as teaching tools and tools for helping students see attributes of quality products can be an essential instructional device for physical education, shop, English composition, speech, or math problem solving. Fostering in students the important life and workplace skills of technology literacy, civil discourse, thinking, writing, reading purposefully, problem solving, researching, and understanding the learning process and various learning styles must be part of the responsibilities assumed by all secondary teachers.

Teaching in block periods provides us more opportunity to teach whole persons, not just subject matter. When a teacher is constrained by a 45- or 50-minute period, the teacher's use of active learning strategies is equally constrained, because active learning takes time. Block periods offer larger chunks of time, which students need if they are to be actively involved as learners. The IC can play an important role as a second head helping teachers use the abovementioned skills as vehicles to deliver their content and to engage students actively in learning it.

3. With how many teachers and schools is it reasonable or practical to expect an instructional coach to work?

Team-teaching at two of the district institutes developed for me a context for work with teachers from all three secondary schools. Juggling my three buildings with 130 total staff, my central office responsibilities as the only secondary member of the C and I team, and my out-of-district duties made me like the old woman who lived in the shoe. An IC cannot reach all teachers and cannot be responsible for saving really marginal teachers. To affect classroom instruction for as many students as possible, I was advised that my job was to assist proficient teachers as they moved along the Tahoma District's teacher developmental continuum. It is comforting to remember that a ripple effect occurs as each teacher I affect has an impact on those around him/her. I also discovered that some teachers never seek help because they either direct their own development or are interested primarily in maintaining a comfortable status quo with their familiar instructional strategies.

Working as in IC at three secondary schools kept me insanely busy. No such position had existed before, so teachers and principals greatly appreciated my support in their buildings. From my perspective, the demands on my time and energy as teachers began to value my services would justify assigning a separate IC to each school. I'd expect that as teachers and principals worked with a school-based IC, they would become increasingly creative in their ability to use the services such a coach could provide.

In the interests of taming my job next year, the first responsibility I will trim from my workload is out-of-district teaching. Though interdistrict networking is valuable, my in-district duties are such that they demand vast energy and coordinating efforts. Each commitment to high schools outside of our district requires hours of preliminary collaboration and preparation, then hours more of travel and actual teaching. Next year I will leave this job of interdistrict networking to someone else.

4. How important is the position of an instructional coach when schools wish to change teachers' instructional practices in block periods?

From the perspective of teachers, an instructional coach's role is a key element when districts wish to change instructional practice in the classroom. Teachers strongly believed a warm, approachable, affirming, and friendly personality in an IC and a wealth of classroom experience to be three times as important as an IC's preparation in the same discipline taught by the teacher being coached. Additionally, willingness to team-teach or master teach was an important quality for an IC to possess.

From the perspective of administrators, though my final questionnaire from them netted sketchy answers, their eagerness to use the energies of the IC throughout the year to head special projects and facilitate inservices indicated commitment to the importance of this position. When interviewed by the head of Curriculum and Instruction in February and again in May as a part of my evaluation, principals spoke enthusiastically about how the presence of an IC in their school made them feel far more connected to the district's educational mission.

Common instructional themes and lesson design formats appear in all of the Tahoma School District's work with professional development: 1) infusion of the six district outcomes into the curriculum at both elementary and secondary (appendix H); 2) the use of thinking skills and graphic organizers to embed content material; 3) direct teaching of Art Costa's Intelligent Behaviors (appendix I); 4) a conscious infusion of the Washington State Essential Learnings (the state's curriculum framework) in new lessons; 5) project-based learning and integrating the curriculum, especially with writing, oral communication, and technology; 6) the use of multiple intelligences and cooperative learning as part of the repertoire of instructional strategies; 7) the regular use of active learning strategies in classroom practice; and 8) incorporation of pre- and postassessments and assessments that are performance-based. The appearance of these common instructional themes in the three district-sponsored institutes, and the support of these through the work done by the IC, provided administrators with additional confidence that the district, the Curriculum and Instruction team, and the instructional coaches were all on the same page and disseminating consistent information.

The following quotes were collected from teachers throughout the year:

> "The presence of an IC provided me the best help I've been given in 15 years."

> "The presence of an IC takes the isolation out of planning and makes teachers more deliberate, thus raising their expectations for students."

> "The visibility and accessibility of the IC makes a big difference."

"The IC nurtures communication between departments, schools, and even between staff members."

"The IC's repertoire of instructional strategies for individual and large-group processing enhanced my repertoire and my planning."

"Having a second head around to bounce ideas off of is important to effective planning."

"I have never worked in a district where staff was as supported as they are in this district. With this nurturing I have grown more this year than in the other 20 years."

"It was good to encounter the ICs at the district institute and have an opportunity to plan one on one with them."

"I appreciated the IC helping me draft my grant proposals."

"A scheduled debriefing with the IC of what I learned at the Instructional Strategies Institute made me feel valued by the district and helped solidify my learning."

"The best part of this job is the opportunity to engage in meaningful conversation with other thoughtful adults."

"I learned more practical classroom ideas in the New Secondary Staff Inservice done for us by the IC in August than I learned in my education classes at my university. I also appreciated the kicked-back atmosphere, conversation about our challenges, and the cool handouts the IC provided at our three Austin Chase coffee house meetings throughout the year."

5. How does an instructional coach develop rapport and trust with teachers?

Here the messages I received from teachers were clear and straightforward:

- Be available.
- Be responsive to teachers' requests and needs.
- Be genuinely helpful. Have specific ideas and tools to offer.
- Be trustworthy and fair.
- Be able to model what you preach.
- Have a sense of humor.

Conclusion

For the IC to be an effective vehicle for change in classroom instructional practice, the IC must be present, accessible, and highly visible in the schools. Because my assignment required me to be at three different schools and the district office, I spent no more than 10 hours in the year isolated in an office. Instead, my car contained materials I used frequently so I could quickly connect instructors to hard copies or models for them to customize for themselves. I began my first year as an instructional coach with the strong doubts common among veteran teachers about the effectiveness of large-group inservices, but I ended the year committed to seeing whole-group work as one tool an IC must use occasionally. What I learned is that whole-group sessions can be very useful if they are connected to an array of additional coaching contexts in which the IC works with teachers, drawing on the content from the whole-group session and helping teachers personalize its application to their classrooms. Being pulled reluctantly into planning and teaching district-sponsored institutes in assessment and active learning instruction, I came to appreciate these as effective and essential links to changing classroom practices. Initially, I felt uncertain about helping science, math, or physical education instructors, but I became convinced that solid instruction has common characteristics that transcend content boundaries.

Another important confirmation my research provided was that collaboration and planning with other instructors leads to richer products for students. Teaching with another teacher or model teaching in another teacher's classroom reveals subtleties of the craft that are best taught through demonstration, modeling, and then discussion in shared reflection about the process. Serving as a courier for exciting practices that I discovered through visiting classrooms around the district builds rapport by affirming the efforts of teachers and provides a network to share expertise that otherwise would be confined to a limited audience. In addition, part of my success in this position as an instructional coach was that I continued to receive a teacher's salary, plus seven additional paid days. When my fellow teachers commented, "Well, Liz, into the big bucks now?" I was open about receiving the same salary I had as a teacher. I was one of their colleagues with more experience teaching and with a strong belief that each of us could work better in collaboration than in isolation. Seeing my role as that of instructional coach instead of master teacher kept this essential collaborative tenor in our relationships.

Block periods are the death of winging it. No longer can teachers plan in the parking lot for the first-period class. No longer can they lecture or show a film all period. Districts moving into block periods should seriously consider the position of an instructional coach as a key part of changing instruction at the classroom level. As a prerequisite to hiring for such a position, or even writing a job description for such a position, I would make reading and talking about this action research project a requirement.

Reference

Harmin, M. (1994). *Inspiring active learning*. Alexandria, VA: Association for Supervision and Curriculum Development.

Appendix A

Work Sites and Responsibilities

Glacier Park School—Grade 7

Principal job site—1st semester

- Work at site a minimum of four hours daily
- Consult bimonthly with principal to determine staff, curriculum, special project needs.
- Consult with staff individually to determine instructional needs.
- Drop in often to classrooms to remind staff of my presence in building, to provide on-the-spot input on instruction, to understand individual teaching styles and the seventh grade habits of mind.
- Consult with individual teachers during their planning periods, lunch breaks, before and after school.
- Read, read, read curriculum support materials and connect these to staff.

Special Year—Long Projects

- Plan and present two half-day inservices to whole staff.
- Support the development of Literature Circles for block teachers:
  — Select, arrange for reading 16 fiction titles focused on Asia, Africa, Mid-East themes.
  — Develop and teach delivery and organizational strategies for Literature Circle work.
- Begin a focus group of teachers to study eighth period:
  — Help write grant.
  — Help survey students/staff on changes needed in eighth period.
  — Organize summer work to clarify practices in eighth period.
- Work with math department to integrate lessons into Asia, Africa, Mid-East units and themes.
- Work with NWIFTL group on their resubmission grant.
- Contact, then work with guest speaker to infuse active learning themes and math into her Kenya presentation.
- Network cross-age teaching between high school and seventh grade school.
- Work with Assessment and Instructional Strategies Institute participants.

TJHS/THSE—Grades 8, 9

Principal job site—2nd semester

- Work at site and be highly visible thirty hours a month first semester.
- Conduct a survey of staff instructional interests.
- Consult with the principals to determine staff, curriculum, special project needs.
- Work at site a minimum of four hours daily second semester.
- Drop in often to classrooms to remind staff of my presence in building, to provide on-the-spot input on instruction, to familiarize myself with teacher styles and eighth and ninth grade habits of mind.
- Consult with individual teachers during their planning periods, lunch breaks, before and after school.

Special Projects

- Plan and present two half-day inservices to whole staff.
- Provide mentor teacher support to three new teachers as part of the district's Mentor Teacher Program.
- Provide math teachers Writing-in-Math materials.
- Survey, foster discussions, arrange summer work schedule for special projects: science, eighth period, Reader Response Groups.
- Support the new ninth grade integrated team.
- Work with special education teachers on infusing active learning strategies into their inservice presentation.
- Work with Assessment and Instructional Strategies Institutes participants.

Tahoma High School—Grades 9–12

- Dismantle classroom of 29 years and select, organize, and distill materials that have broad applicability to generic classroom use.
- Review, revise, reformat a classroom handbook for Civil Discourse on five levels.
- Consult with principal to determine staff, curriculum, and special project needs.
- Work with individual teachers on-site four hours/week (English, math, social studies, family and consumer science, science departments).
- Work with Assessment and Instructional Strategies Institute participants.

Special Year—Long Projects

- Continue work with integrated 11.
  - — Organize, schedule, and facilitate English and social studies instructors to plan this class integrating U.S. History with English 11 (September through July).
  - — Draft, revise, present proposal to school board.
- Assume responsibility for coordinating, scheduling, facilitating, drafting NWIFTL Grant activities (September to May).

- Work with students and teachers developing programs for cross-age teaching.
- Work with American Expressions eleventh grade teachers to revise and redraft oral history project to imitate and rehearse senior project format.
- Work with teachers to define and extend Service Learning as a secondary curriculum component.
- Continue work with the Senior Project refinement.

Central Office/Out-of-District Duties

- Participate in Curriculum and Instruction team meetings each Monday morning.
- Attend National Faculty meetings as a central office support person for district participants.
- Attend an administrative retreat.
- Meet with home school coordinator (September to June).
- Plan and team-teach New Teacher Orientation.
- Plan and solo teach New Secondary Teacher Orientation.
- Plan and facilitate new secondary teachers coffeehouse talk sessions (×3).
- Meet six times a year with the district Staff Development Steering Committee.
- Teach active learning strategies for block periods at out-of-district high schools (×8).
- Design, disseminate, assist teachers in writing Tahoma Teacher Grants.
- Plan and team-teach Tahoma Assessment Training Institute for math and reading, 40 hours (September to December).
- Attend Mentor Teacher programs.
- Chair, schedule, and facilitate the district Writing Steering Committee meetings (×5).
- Plan and team-teach Tahoma Instructional Strategies Institute (October to April).
- Attend as a student Cognitive Coaching class (six days).
- Write Service Learning Grant, secondary focus.
- Attend NWIFTL Grant activities (six days September to May).
- Teach Literacy Strand class for Tahoma District.
- Meet with secondary health curriculum coordinator.
- Plan and facilitate summer committee work in math, art, science, health, block classes, eighth period, and Secondary Staff Development NWIFTL Grant.

Appendix B

Measurement Tools

Researcher Journal—This journal is a place where I reflect on my practice of being an instructional coach. It is a running record of teachers helped, practices recommended or designed, the physical setting of the encounter, the duration of the encounter (was assistance given on the fly in the hallway or local supermarket, or was the meeting scheduled), and follow-up conversation.

Questionnaire for Teachers

This questionnaire is designed to help the instructional coach reflect on the effectiveness of his/her practices. For the purpose of clarity: An instructional coach (IC) is an experienced educator current with educational research and skilled in the use of active learning strategies. The IC has been assigned to the building as a resource person to assist instructors in building their teaching repertoires for block periods.

1. Has the IC assisted you in your instructional planning?   ＿＿＿ Yes   ＿＿＿ No
   How often? Once or twice ＿＿＿ three to four times ＿＿＿ several times ＿＿＿
   Briefly describe the nature of his/her help.

2. Have your meetings with the instructional coach been scheduled, formal
   meetings or unscheduled, informal meetings?＿＿＿＿＿＿＿＿＿＿＿＿＿＿＿＿＿＿
   Place ＿＿＿＿＿＿＿＿＿＿＿＿＿＿＿＿＿＿＿＿＿＿＿＿＿＿＿＿＿＿＿＿＿＿＿＿＿＿
   Length of encounter: ＿＿＿ 10 to 15 min. ＿＿＿ 1 to 2 hrs. ＿＿＿ 2 to 3 hrs.
   ＿＿＿ Formal Inservice
   Which of these meetings is most valuable?＿＿＿＿＿＿＿＿＿＿＿＿＿＿＿＿＿＿＿
   Why?＿＿＿＿＿＿＿＿＿＿＿＿＿＿＿＿＿＿＿＿＿＿＿＿＿＿＿＿＿＿＿＿＿＿＿＿＿＿

3. Referring to the definition of an instructional coach, has your teaching repertoire for block periods been expanded by the presence of an IC?
   Explain ＿＿＿＿＿＿＿＿＿＿＿＿＿＿＿＿＿＿＿＿＿＿＿＿＿＿＿＿＿＿＿＿＿＿＿＿

4. How valuable is the position of an IC in enhancing instructional practices for teachers?
   Of Little Use ＿＿＿   Important ＿＿＿
   Explain ＿＿＿＿＿＿＿＿＿＿＿＿＿＿＿＿＿＿＿＿＿＿＿＿＿＿＿＿＿＿＿＿＿＿＿＿

5. Has student learning in your classroom been affected by the presence of an IC in the building? Please consider degree of student engagement with the assignment(s), quality of student products, effectiveness of the suggestions from the IC on student motivation, and engagement.

    _____

6. Which of the listed attributes is most important in an IC? Please number in order of importance.
    _____ Classroom experience
    _____ Knowledge of current research and practice
    _____ Personality
    _____ Availability
    _____ Skill with cognitive coaching
    _____ Willingness to team-teach or master-teach
    _____ Preparation in my discipline

7. From your perspective, what is the most efficient use of an IC?
    _____ Whole-faculty inservice
    _____ Focused study groups self-selected by participants
    _____ Informal, unscheduled encounters
    _____ Scheduled, assisted planning time
    _____ Disseminator of instructional and professional growth articles
    _____ Team teacher
    _____ Master teacher demonstrating practices

Questionnaire for Administrators

#'s 3, 4, 6, 7 from above questionnaire

Appendix C

Tahoma School District

Staff Preworkshop Assessment Tool

The purpose of this tool is to assess the expertise and knowledge of a staff prior to an inservice day. The following areas are important elements of instruction in the Tahoma School District.

Please respond to the following prompts:

1. District Outcomes
   - List the 6 outcomes.

   _____   _____

   _____   _____

   _____   _____

   - Are the outcomes posted in your teaching area? _____ Yes   _____ No
   - Do you teach directly to these outcomes? _____ Yes   _____ No
   - Describe here one activity you use in your classroom that specifically supports the outcomes.

   _____

   _____

   _____

2. Thinking Skills/Graphic Organizers
   List 5 of the 20 thinking skills and the accompanying graphic organizer you use regularly in your classroom.

   _____

   _____

   _____

3. Intelligent Behaviors (Costa)
   List 4 of the 12 intelligent behaviors you stress in your discipline.

   _____

   _____

   _____

Describe how you teach to one of these behaviors in your class.

_____

_____

_____

4. Integrating the Curriculum
   • Have you participated in formal training?   _____ Yes   _____ No
   Describe how that training has influenced decisions you make in your class-room.

   _____

   _____

   _____

5. Multiple Intelligences
   • I use the multiple intelligences as part of my instructional strategies.
         seldom   ◄————————►   often
   • List Howard Gardner's seven intelligences

   _____

   _____

   _____

   _____

   • Describe two of the activities you use to incorporate the multiple intelligences into your delivery model.

   _____

   _____

   _____

6. Cooperative Learning
   • I use cooperative learning in my classroom.
         seldom   ◄————————►   often
   • List here the operating principles that must be in place for this complex process to work.

   _____

   _____

   _____

   _____

7. Active Learning Strategies
   * Describe here 5 active learning strategies you frequently use to engage your students in instruction.

   _____

   _____

   _____

8. Assessment
   * Describe 3 ways you measure student understanding.

   _____

   _____

   _____

9. What additional half-day inservice training would you appreciate?
   ____ State Essential Learnings   ____ Classroom Management
   ____ District Outcomes   ____ Multiple Intelligences
   ____ Thinking Skills/Graphic Organizers   ____ Cooperative Learning
   ____ Intelligent Behaviors   ____ Active Learning
   ____ Integrating the Curriculum   ____ Assessment
   ____ Other instructional strategies that can be inserviced on half-days and encourage collaborative growth among staff members.

   _____

   _____

   _____

10. What instructional strategy expertise would you be willing to teach on half-days to the staff?

   _____

   _____

   _____

Appendix D

Active Learning Folder

An Organization of Materials to Engage Students in Learning

We learn and retain about 10 percent of what we hear.

We learn and retain about 15 percent of what we see.

We learn and retain about 20 percent of what we both see and hear.

We learn and retain about 40 percent of what we discuss with others.

We learn and retain about 60 percent of what we do or experience.

We learn and retain about 90 percent of what we teach someone else.

— *J. E. Slice, 1984*

A Menu of Teacher Choices for Lesson Designing*

☐ Lesson Design Tools

☐ Washington State Essential Learnings

☐ District Outcomes

☐ Thinking Skills and Graphic Organizers

☐ Writing to Deepen Understanding

☐ Cooperative Grouping

☐ Multiple Intelligences

☐ Assessment/Testing Designs

☐ Discussion Strategies

☐ Active Learning for Film and Video

☐ A Design for Group Research

☐ Questioning Strategies to Extend Thinking

☐ Building a Community of Learners

☐ Negotiation Process

☐ Truths about Learning

☐ Intelligent Behaviors

☐ Learning Styles

☐ Brain Research

*Plan three to five activities per period to keep momentum and deliver your content.

Appendix E

Class 30 Compilation—A Collection of Practical Vehicles to Carry Content

Table of Contents

Section One:	*Building a classroom atmosphere for a community of learners*
	Truth Signs
	A Negotiation Process
	Cultivating Couth
	Intelligent Behaviors
	Active Learning Strategies List
	Two Lesson Design Formats
	Assessments Overview
	Two Rubrics: Visual Aids, Oral Presentations
	Learning Styles Self-Assessments
	Thinking Skills Checklist
Section Two:	*Cooperative learning*
	The Big Picture (rules for, how it looks, operating principles for success)
	Task Analysis Model for Working Effectively in Cooperative Groups
Section Three:	*Multiple intelligences*
Section Four:	*Involving students with reading*
	Clear Seeing—A Tool for Reading Nonfiction
	Fiction Reading Tool
	Values Sort (personal values sheet; national values sheet)
	Book Group Book Mark
	Responding after Reading a Book
	Poetic Devices
	Cooperative Reading Groups (in progress activities; concluding activities)
	Characters in Crypts
	Poetic Images

Appendix F

Active Learning Strategies

We learn and retain about 10 percent of what we hear.
We learn and retain about 15 percent of what we see.
We learn and retain about 20 percent of what we both see and hear.
We learn and retain about 40 percent of what we discuss with others.
We learn and retain about 60 percent of what we do or experience.
We learn and retain about 90 percent of what we teach someone else.
(J. E. Slice, 1984)

☐ Mind mapping

☐ SSR with Post-it® Notes

☐ Pair share

☐ Whip around, pass (small group, large group)

☐ Critical questioning

☐ Learning logs

☐ Jigsaw (expert groups)

☐ Pantomime

☐ Cooperative learning groups

☐ Role-playing simulations

☐ Sketching (concretes and abstracts)

☐ Story spinning

☐ Jewelers loupes

☐ Graphic organizers

☐ Self-reflection prompts

☐ Lecture listings

☐ Job cards

☐ Relay raps

☐ Metaphor making

Appendix G

Active Learning Strategies Especially Useful in Math Classrooms

(Many of these strategies are described in detail in *Inspiring Active Learning: A Handbook for Teachers*, Harmin, Merill. Alexandria VA: Association for Supervision and Curriculum Development, 1994.)

Pair share (2–5 min.): Tell and show or draw for a partner the essence of what you're learning.

Pair share then questions (2–4 min.): Converse with a partner first; if questions still remain, ask the teacher after you have conversed.

Whip around pass (1–3 min.): Teacher quickly whips around the classroom soliciting learnings from the pairs. (Call on three to six pairs, not all pairs.)

Question, all write (1–4 min.): Whole class responds in writing to a prompt from teacher, then share with a partner, then whip around to some pairs for whole-group sharing.

Outcome sentences (1–3 min.): Students only respond in writing to the prompt or outcome sentence.

Tutor pairs (2–5 min.): Students take turns for a day tutoring (reteaching) a partner new concepts or reviewing old concepts, then the teacher can do a quick WHIP AROUND.

Voting (5 seconds): Show of hands indicating right or wrong.

Attentive lecture (2–4 min., every 10–12 min. during lecture): Using the four-part lecture grid, teacher pauses at key points so students can take notes, then trade notes with a partner to embed understanding or clear up confusion.

Three before me (15 seconds–5 min.): Students seek information from other students before seeking information from the teacher.

Growing curriculum maps (1–4 min.): A cluster outline (on either butcher paper or a transparency) of the class's learnings over a unit. Teacher and students together add to the map at the end of each period and briefly revisit it at the beginning of the next period. Might be made available for use on tests.

World warmups: Five-minute warm-up exercises provided by teacher (yes, there are books of short, visually inviting problems ready for putting on a transparency) or by student pairs, of math from the world of sports, advertising, general news, trends. These math warm-ups do not have to be subject-specific to be of value.

Create you own homework: Challenge students to invent unique homework applications of concepts they are studying.

Appendix H

Outcomes and Indicators

Tahoma School District, Maple Valley, Washington

I. Self-Directed Learners
    A. Set goals
    B. Persistence
    C. Decision maker
    D. Reflective and evaluative
    E. Inquisitive

II. Collaborative Workers
    A. Sharing
    B. Empathy and respect
    C. Active listener
    D. Flexible
    E. Encouraging

III. Effective Communicators
     A. Clarity of expression
     B. Range of methods: multiple intelligences
     C. Technologically literate
     D. Responsive to diverse audiences
     E. Interprets and evaluates

IV. Community Contributors
    A. Provide service
    B. Harmonious
    C. Future-oriented
    D. Improve welfare of others
    E. Enhances the environment

V. Quality Producers
    A. High standards
    B. Reflects originality
    C. Uses a variety of resources
    D. Aesthetically pleasing
    E. Criteria-based

VI. Complex Thinkers
   A. Creative
   B. Problem-solver
   C. Risk-taker
   D. Analytical
   E. Metacognitive

Appendix I

Intelligent Behaviors

Attending   Focuses on the task at hand; is not easily distracted

Persistence   Keeps on trying; does not give up easily

Deliberateness   Shows less impulsivity; thinks before acting

Flexibility   Open to alternatives; sees many possibilities

Precision   Uses words carefully; checks for accuracy, attends to detail

Inquisitiveness   Asks questions; enjoys problem solving; is curious

Fluency   Can generate many different ideas

Originality   Enjoys making and doing original things

Metacognition   Puts into words his/her own thinking; self-reflects

Empathy   Listens to others with sensitivity and understanding

Elaboration   Builds on other people's thinking

Risking   Willing to take on new challenges; not afraid of making mistakes

About the Author

David Marshak is an associate professor in the School of Education at Seattle University. He teaches primarily in a preservice Master in Teaching Program. He has served as a teacher of students of all ages, a consultant and curriculum developer, and a district coordinator of curriculum, assessment, and school restructuring. His research interests include teaching and learning in block periods, multiage elementary programs, and the efficacy of small, personalized schools.